funky
chunky

knitted accessories

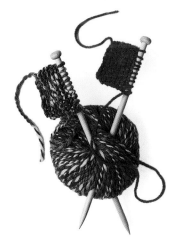

funky
chunky
knitted accessories

jan eaton

Martingale®
& COMPANY

Conceived and produced by
Breslich & Foss Ltd., London

Volume © Breslich & Foss Ltd., 2006
Text: **Jan Eaton**
Photography: **Martin Norris**
Design: **Elizabeth Healey**
Project Management: **Janet Ravenscroft**

First American edition published by
Martingale & Company
20205 144th Ave. NE
Woodinville, WA 98072-8478 USA
www.martingale-pub.com

Martingale®
& C O M P A N Y

Printed in China

11 10 09 08 07 06   6 5 4 3 2 1

Library of Congress Cataloging-in-
Publication Data is available upon request.

ISBN: 1-56477-647-6

Mission Statement
*Dedicated to providing quality products and
service to inspire creativity.*

contents

introduction

Taking a range of five easy-to-make knitting patterns as a starting point, we show you how to turn a simple accessory into something wonderfully individual. By crafting edgings and trimmings, fastenings, handles, and a wide range of embellishments and combining them with chunky knitting, you can create items that are truly unique.

Begin by checking the Basic Techniques section on pages 8 to 24. Here you'll find all the information you need to take up the craft of knitting and quickly become proficient with yarn and needles. Each technique is presented in an easy-to-understand sequence of instructions illustrated with close-up photographs that will help you every step of the way.

Once you've become familiar with basic knitting skills, try out some of the basic patterns on pages 25 to 27. Whether you want to make a scarf, hat, bag, pair of mittens, or a capelet, you'll find these basic accessories are easy to knit. If you can handle casting on, working knit stitches, and binding off, you're ready to make your first scarf. As your skills and confidence improve with practice, try the basic hat and bag, then go on to make the mittens and capelet.

Delving into the next three chapters you can begin to express yourself and have some real fun! Drawing on a wealth of decorative ideas and suggestions, there are over 60 inspiring accessories based on the five basic patterns. To make it easy to find your way round the book, the designs are divided into three sections. Edgings and Trimmings,

pages 28 to 51, concentrates on different types of edgings and trimmings including fringes, pompoms, hem variations, appliqué, and tassels. Fastenings and Handles, pages 52 to 75, shows you how to make and attach different styles of handles and closures including ties, braids, tabs with buckles, zippers, and ribbon bows. Beading and Embellishing, page 76 to 99, goes wild with buttons, beads, bells, and charms. Here you'll discover how to add glitz with beads, stitch embellishments onto your knitting, and make your own knitted buttons.

The final chapter, Customizing Knitting on pages 100 to 115 contains inspiring suggestions and helpful hints for doing something a little bit different with your knitting. This chapter shows you how to improvise your own variations of basic patterns, work with different stitch patterns, and incorporate novelty yarns. It also covers coming to grips with easy washing-machine felting, working embroidery on knitting, and knitting with recycled fabrics.

At the back of the book, starting on page 116, you'll find an illustrated Gallery, which contains a photograph of every accessory and variation in the book. The designs are arranged by item so that all the same type of accessory are shown together. Browse through the pictures and enjoy deciding what to make for your next knitting project.

jan eaton

chapter 1
basic techniques and patterns

This introductory section contains everything you need to know to get started in the craft of knitting. From **choosing and handling yarns** and needles to blocking finished pieces, and from joining a new yarn to making up the accessories, all the essentials are shown here in clear step-by-step photographs. Once you have mastered the art of knitting and purling, turn to the **Basic Patterns** on page 25. Here you'll find instructions for making the **Buttonhole Bag**, **Scarf**, **Mittens**, **Hat,** and **Capelet**.

Materials

A ball of chunky yarn, a pair of knitting needles, and a basic sewing kit are all you need to get started with this fascinating craft. Yarn and needles come in a variety of weights, materials, and sizes: the information in this section will help you choose which to buy.

YARN

Each project in the book can be knitted with your own choice of yarn. As well as using different colors, fiber composition is also a choice you have to make. Many knitters prefer to use pure wool yarns, but there are times when synthetic yarns are preferable, particularly for items that require frequent washing. Wool yarns are generally more expensive than wool/synthetic blends and those made entirely from synthetics. You may prefer to use a pure cotton or synthetic/cotton blend yarn as these are less itchy than some made from wool.

You can also be adventurous and incorporate some textured yarns, such as mohair, tweed, or ribbon yarn in your accessory, but try to combine yarns of similar weight. As an alternative to chunky weight yarns, you can use finer weights and knit with two or more strands together to make a thicker yarn. The scarf on page 110 is knit with two yarn strands; one is smooth and the other is a textured eyelash yarn.

Novelty and solid-colored chunky weight yarns

Chunky weight yarn

Novelty ribbon yarn

Suggestions for yarn combinations

To make up a chunky yarn weight, try combining:

• Three strands of sport weight (4ply) yarn.

• Two strands of double knitting (DK) yarn.

• One strand of worsted weight (Aran) yarn plus one of sport weight (4ply) yarn.

Two strands of double knitting weight yarn

One strand of worsted weight yarn plus one strand of sport weight yarn

Three strands of sport weight yarn

NEEDLES

The basic knitting tool is a pair of needles. Single-pointed, straight knitting needles come in a range of sizes from small (US size 0/2 mm) to large (US size 19/15 mm) to suit different weights of yarn. Straight needles are made from aluminum, wood, bamboo, or different types of plastic and they are usually available in two lengths: 10 and 14 inch. (25 and 36 cm). Choose whichever type of needle feels best in your hands and is comfortable to use.

Ball bands

The ball band—or paper tag on knitting yarn—has lots of useful information printed on it, including the fiber content of the yarn, its weight, and the yardage of the ball or skein. Some bands also include suggested needle sizes and gauge measurements, as well as washing or dry-cleaning information.

Useful yarn/needle combinations

Sport weight (4ply) US sizes 3–5 (3.25 to 3.75 mm)

Double knitting (DK) US sizes 5–7 (3.75 to 4 mm)

Worsted weight (Aran) US sizes 7–9 (4 to 5.5 mm)

Chunky weight (Chunky) US sizes 9–11 (5.5 to 8 mm)

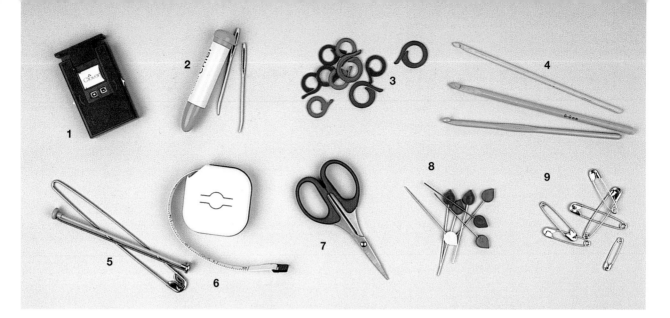

KNITTING EQUIPMENT

1 Use a **row counter** to keep track of the number of rows you work.

2 Yarn **needles** with blunt tips and large eyes are available in a range of sizes to suit different yarn weights.

3 Use a **stitch marker** to mark your place. Split coil markers like these are better than solid rings: they can be slipped from needle to needle or attached directly into a stitch.

4 Keep one or two **crochet hooks** in different sizes handy to pick up dropped stitches.

5 Available in different shapes and sizes, **stitch holders** hold groups of stitches that will be worked later in the pattern.

6 Buy a retractable **tape measure** that has both imperial and metric measurements. Fiberglass tapes are more accurate because they do not stretch.

7 Buy a small pair of **scissors** with sharp points. If you want to keep scissors in your knitting bag, buy a pair with a sheath or put a plastic point protector over the points.

8 Glass- or plastic-headed **pins** are easy to see and don't slip through knitted fabric. Use ordinary dressmaking pins or buy special marking ones that are longer.

9 Safety pins are invaluable for catching and holding dropped stitches before they ladder or run.

Optional equipment

A set of plastic pompom forms are useful for making different sizes of pompoms. A wooden knitting nancy (or knitting spool) is also useful, enabling you to make tubular cords for fastening or trimming accessories. A notebook and pencil are handy for jotting down rows if you don't have a row counter. Don't put pens in your bag as they may leak and ruin your knitting and yarn.

Common knitting abbreviations

alt – alternate

beg – beginning

BO – bind off

CO – cast on

cont – continue

dec - decrease

foll – following

inc - increase

K – knit

K2tog – knit 2 stitches together

M1 – make 1 extra stitch

P – purl

P2tog – purl 2 stitches together

psso – pass slipped stitch over

rem – remaining

rep – repeat

RS – right side of work

sl – slip next stitch

sl 1, K1, psso – slip 1, knit 1, pass
    slipped stitch over

st(s) – stitch(es)

St st – stockinette stitch

tbl – through back loops

tog - together

WS - wrong side of work

YO – yarn over needle

Holding Yarn and Needles

There is no right or wrong way to hold the yarn and needles when you are knitting: experiment until you find the most comfortable method. Some knitters control the yarn with their right hand by feeding it through and around their fingers. Others control the yarn with the left hand and hold the right needle like a pen.

Pen grip with yarn in right hand

Hold the left needle with your hand over the top and the right needle like a pen, and use your right hand to control the flow of the yarn. Use your right forefinger to make a stitch without letting the needle drop.

Pen grip with yarn in left hand

Hold the left needle with your hand over the top, using the left hand to control the yarn. Hold the right needle like a pen. Hold the yarn taut with your left hand and catch the yarn with the tip of the right needle to make a stitch.

Knife grip with yarn in right hand

Hold the left needle with your hand over the top and the right needle overhand like a knife, and use your right hand to control the flow of the yarn, taking your right hand off the needle to make a stitch. Some knitters tuck the end of the right needle under their right arm, others hold both needles with their left thumb where the points cross.

Knife grip with yarn in left-hand

Hold the left needle with your hand over the top, using the left hand to control the yarn. Hold the right needle like a knife. When making a stitch, hold the yarn taut with your left hand and catch the yarn with the tip of the right needle to make a stitch.

Starting to knit

The first step when starting to knit is to place the required number of stitches on the needle, beginning with a slip knot. This process is called casting on. There are several methods of casting on and each produces a different kind of edge.

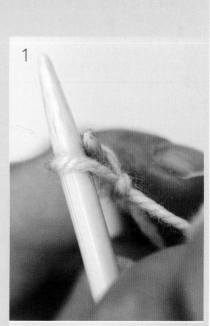

MAKING A SLIP KNOT

Make a slip knot on the left needle to anchor the end of the yarn before casting on the required number of stitches. Make the knot with your fingers, then slip it onto the needle.

1 Pull a short length of yarn from the ball. Make a loose loop of yarn round your first finger.

2 Keeping the first loop intact, push the strand of yarn attached to the ball through the first loop to make a new loop.

3 Slip the loop off your finger. Place the new loop on the needle and tighten both ends of yarn so the loop is pulled close to the needle.

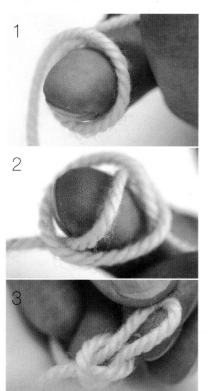

CASTING ON

The cable method is a good way to cast on as it produces a neat edge.

1 Make a slip knot and place it on one needle. Hold the needle with the knot in your left hand with the short yarn end held firmly under your fingers. Take the other needle in your right hand and insert the tip into the loop.

2 Bring the yarn from the ball over the right needle so that it is between the needle points. Use the tip of the right needle to pull a new loop of yarn through the previous loop. Then use the right needle to lift the loop onto the left needle. Tighten the yarn gently. Two stitches are now cast on.

3 Insert the right needle behind the first stitch on the left needle, wrap the yarn over and pull a new loop of yarn through onto the right needle. Place the new loop on the left needle. Repeat this step until you have the number of stitches needed on the left needle. If your cast-on stitches are very tight, it's a good idea to use a left needle one size larger when casting on. This will help prevent a tight edge to your work.

WORKING A ROW OF KNIT STITCHES

The knit stitch is one of two foundation stitches in knitting: knit and purl. When you work every row of knitting in this stitch, the resulting ridged pattern is called garter stitch and the knitted fabric looks the same on both sides. When your final pattern row has been knitted, secure the stitches by binding off as shown on page 19.

1 Hold the needle with the stitches in your left hand. Insert the tip of the right needle into the first stitch and bring the yarn over between the needles with your right hand.

2 Pull the yarn through the stitch with the right needle, and at the same time, slip the original stitch off the left needle.

3 The newly made knit stitch is on the right needle, seen in the foreground. Proceed along the row, making 1 knit stitch on the right needle from every stitch on the left needle. To work the next row, turn the work, hold the needle with the stitches in your left hand and repeat from Step 1.

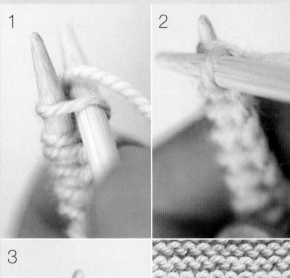

Garter stitch

WORKING A ROW OF PURL STITCHES

Purl stitches are the opposite of knit stitches. The best-known combination of knit and purl stitches is called stockinette stitch, which is made by knitting and purling alternate rows. Knit rows form the smooth right side of stockinette stitch and the purl rows form the ridged wrong side.

1 Holding yarn and needles in the same way as for working knit stitches and with the yarn at the front of the work, insert the tip of the right needle into the front of the first stitch from right to left.

2 Loop yarn around the tip of the right needle.

3 Use the tip of the right needle to draw a loop of yarn through the stitch to make a new stitch on the right needle. Slip the old stitch off the left needle.

4 Proceed along the row, making 1 purl stitch on the right needle from every stitch on the left needle. To work the next row, turn the work, hold the needle with the stitches in your left hand and repeat from Step 1 of Knit Stitches.

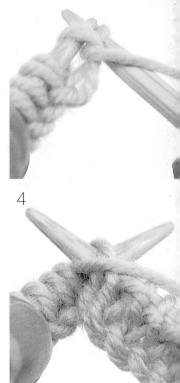

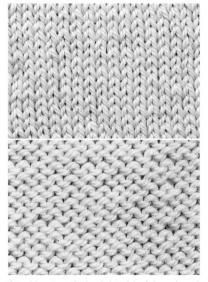

Stockinette stitch: right side (above) and wrong side (below)

WORKING SINGLE RIB

Simple rib patterns are combinations of knit and purl stitches arranged to make stretchy, flexible fabrics that spring back into shape when stretched. This feature makes them ideal for working hats and cuffs. Single rib (also known as 1x1 rib) alternates single knit and purl stitches along the row. It can be worked over an odd or even number of stitches. The example below is worked over an even number of stitches.

1 With the yarn at the back of the work, knit the first stitch on the left needle.

2 Bring the yarn forward to the front of the work between the needles and purl the next stitch on the left needle.

3 Take the yarn to the back of the work between the needles and knit the next stitch. Continue along the row, working alternate knit and purl stitches and changing the position of the yarn after every stitch.

4 On the next and subsequent rows, as the stitches face you, knit the knit stitches and purl the purl stitches.

1

2

3

4

Single rib

WORKING DOUBLE RIB

Double rib (also known as 2x2 rib) alternates pairs of knit and purl stitches. It can be worked only over an even number of stitches, as shown in the example below.

1 With the yarn at the back of the work, knit the first 2 stitches on the left needle.

2 Bring the yarn forward to the front of the work between the needles and purl the next 2 stitches on the left needle.

3 Take the yarn to the back of the work between the needles and knit the next 2 stitches. Continue along the row, working alternate pairs of knit and purl stitches and changing the position of the yarn after every 2 stitches.

4 On the next and subsequent rows, as the stitches face you, knit the knit stitches and purl the purl stitches.

Double rib

WORKING SEED STITCH

Seed stitch is a variation of single rib that makes a fairly thick fabric that lies flat and has an attractive textured surface. Seed stitch can be worked over an odd or an even number of stitches. The example below is worked over an even number of stitches.

1 With the yarn at the back of the work, knit the first stitch on the left needle.

2 Bring the yarn forward to the front of the work between the needles and purl the next stitch on the left needle.

3 Take the yarn to the back of the work between the needles and knit the next stitch. Continue along the row, working alternate knit and purl stitches and changing the position of the yarn after every stitch.

4 On the next and subsequent rows, as the stitches face you, knit the purl stitches and purl the knit stitches.

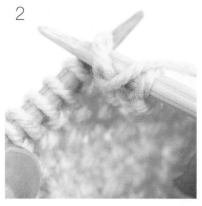

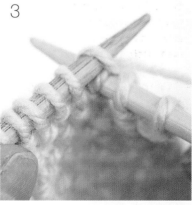

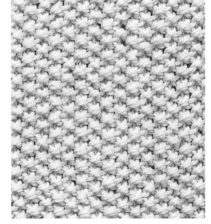

Seed stitch

ALL ABOUT GAUGE

The term "gauge" refers to the number of stitches and rows contained in a given width and length of knit fabric. The patterns in this book include a recommended gauge for the yarn that has been used and it's important that you match this gauge exactly so your work comes out the right size. This is usually quoted as "x stitches and y rows to 4 in. (10 cm)" measured over a certain stitch pattern using a certain size of needles. Gauge can be affected by the type of yarn used, the size and brand of the knitting needles, and the type of stitch pattern. For items such as scarves and bags, getting the correct gauge is less important than when making mittens or hats, where a good fit is crucial.

Making and measuring a gauge sample

Read the pattern instructions to find the recommended gauge. Working in the exact yarn you will use for the item, make a generously sized sample 6–8 in. (15–20 cm) wide. Work in the required pattern until the piece is 6–8 in. (15–20 cm) long. Fasten off the yarn. Block the gauge sample using the method suited to the yarn fiber content (page 23) and allow to dry.

1 Lay the sample right side up on a flat surface and use a ruler or tape measure to measure 4 in. (10 cm) horizontally across a row of stitches. Mark this measurement by inserting 2 pins exactly 4 in. (10 cm) apart. Make a note of the number of stitches (including partial stitches) between the pins. This is the number of stitches to 4 in. (10 cm).

2 Turn the sample on its side. Working in the same way, measure 4 in. (10 cm) across the rows, again inserting 2 pins exactly 4 in. (10 cm) apart. Make a note of the number of rows (including partial rows) between the pins. This is the number of rows to 4 in. (10 cm).

How to adjust the gauge

If you have more stitches or rows between the pins inserted in your gauge sample, your gauge is too tight and you should make another sample using needles one size larger. If you have fewer stitches or rows between the pins, your gauge is too loose and you should make another sample using needles one size smaller. Block the new sample and measure the gauge as before. Repeat this process until your gauge matches that given in the pattern.

JOINING A NEW YARN

When you have used up your first ball of yarn, you need to join in the next ball. Always join the new yarn at the beginning of a row to avoid holes appearing in your knitting. Use this method for joining a different color of yarn, for example, when working a striped pattern.

1 Tie the new yarn around the end of the old yarn, using an overhand knot and leaving a tail of about 6 in. (15 cm).

2 Tighten the knot and push it up close to the edge of the work ready to make the first stitch of the new row.

3 Work the new row using the new ball of yarn. When the knitting is finished, undo the knot and weave in the yarn ends.

DEALING WITH YARN ENDS

Thread the end of the yarn in a large yarn needle. Weave the end through several stitches on the wrong side of the work. Trim the remaining yarn.

MAKING A BUTTONHOLE

Working a 1-row horizontal buttonhole is the neatest way to make any size of buttonhole and has the advantage of not needing any reinforcing. You can make buttonholes on either a right-side row as shown, or on a wrong-side row.

1 Work along the row to the position indicated on the pattern, bring the yarn forward to the front of the work and slip the next stitch purlwise to the right needle without knitting it. Return the yarn to the back of the work.

2 Slip the next stitch on the left needle and pass the first slipped stitch over it and off the right needle to bind off 1 stitch.

3 Repeat Step 2 for the number of times indicated in the pattern. Here, the step has been repeated 3 times more and 4 stitches have been bound off. Slip the last bound-off stitch from the right needle back onto the left needle and turn the work.

4 Keeping the yarn at the back, cast on the number of stitches indicated in the pattern, and turn. This is usually 1 more stitch than the total number of stitches bound off in Steps 2 and 3. Turn the work.

5 Keeping the yarn at the back, slip the first stitch from the left needle onto the right needle. Pass the first cast-on stitch over the slipped stitch and off the needle to close the buttonhole. Work to the end of the row.

1

2

3

4

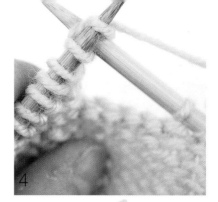

5

BINDING OFF

When your final pattern row has been knitted, bind off the stitches to prevent them from unraveling.

Knit the first 2 stitches on the left needle in the usual way. Insert the left needle into the first stitch on the right needle and lift it over the second stitch and off the needle. Knit the next stitch on the left needle and repeat until there is 1 stitch left on the right needle. Cut the yarn, leaving a 6 in. (15 cm) tail, and pull it through the last stitch to finish.

USING A STITCH HOLDER

A stitch holder is a useful piece of knitting equipment that lets you remove some of the working stitches from the needle and hold them safely out of the way until they are needed. If you don't have a stitch holder at hand, use a spare piece of yarn instead as shown in Steps 3 and 4.

1 Open the stitch holder. Slip the point of the holder into the first stitch on the left needle and carefully ease it off the needle and onto the bar of the holder.

2 Repeat Step 1 until the correct number of stitches have been transferred to the holder as shown. Close the holder so the stitches are held securely then continue knitting across the stitches still on the needle. When the stitches on the holder are needed, transfer them from the holder back onto the knitting needle in the same way.

3 When no stitch holder is available, use a length of contrasting yarn to hold the stitches. Use a yarn needle to thread the yarn through the stitches, taking them off the needle and onto the yarn one by one.

4 When the correct number of stitches has been transferred, knot the yarn ends to make a large loop. When the stitches are needed, undo the knot and carefully slip the stitches back onto the knitting needle.

WORKING INTO THE BACK OF STITCHES

The front of each stitch is always the loop closest to you on the left needle, whether you are working right- or wrong-side rows. Unless stated in the pattern instructions, always work into the front loop of the stitch. When instructed to work into the back loop, work a knit stitch as shown below.

1 To knit into the back loop of a stitch, insert the tip of the right needle behind the left needle and into the loop of the first stitch on the needle.

2 Wrap the yarn over the right needle and knit this loop in the usual way, and then slip it off the left needle.

SLIPPING STITCHES

Many patterns tell you to slip 1 or more stitches. This is done by passing the slipped stitches from the left to the right needle without actually working them. Stitches can be slipped knitwise or purlwise.

1 To slip a stitch knitwise, insert the tip of the right needle into the next stitch on the left needle as if you were going to knit the stitch. Pull this stitch off the left needle without knitting it. The stitch is now on the right needle.

2 To slip a stitch purlwise, insert the tip of the right needle into the next stitch on the left needle as if you were going to purl the stitch. Pull this stitch off the left needle without purling it. The stitch is now on the right needle.

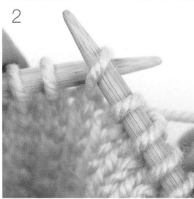

WORKING INCREASES AND DECREASES

Increases and decreases alter the number of stitches on the needle in any given row. They are used to shape a piece of knitting and also for knitting a lace pattern. When shaping knitting, increases and decreases are usually worked 1 or 2 stitches in from the edge of the knitting rather than on the edge as this gives a neater finish.

Working a make-one increase

One extra stitch is worked into the horizontal strand of yarn between 2 ordinary knit stitches. Knit through the back loop of the strand to avoid a small hole forming and make an almost invisible increase.

1 Knit to the position of the increase. Insert the tip of the right needle from front to back into the strand of yarn between the last stitch worked and the first stitch on the left needle.

2 Using the right needle, carefully lift the strand and place it on the left needle to form a loop of yarn. Then remove the right needle.

3 Knit the strand through the back loop (see page 20) and slip the loop off the left needle to make a new stitch on the right needle. One stitch has been increased.

Working a yarn over

A yarn over is a decorative increase used in making lace patterns. It is made by wrapping the yarn around the right needle. The simplest type of yarn over is made between 2 knit stitches on a right side row and this is the only type used in this book.

1 Work to the point indicated in the pattern. To work the yarn over, bring the yarn between the needles from back to front of the work. Wrap the yarn over the right needle. Hold it in place with your forefinger.

2 Knit the next stitch in the usual way. The yarn forms an extra stitch and makes a neat eyelet hole.

3 On the next (wrong-side) row, purl the yarn overs in the same way as the ordinary stitches.

Working a basic right-slanting decrease

Knitting 2 stitches together on a right-side row is the simplest way of decreasing 1 stitch. This method of decreasing is called a single right-slanting decrease as the finished decrease slants to the right on the knit side of the work.

1 Work to the point indicated in the pattern. Insert the tip of the right needle from front to back into the next 2 stitches on the left needle as if you were going to knit.

2 Take the yarn around the needle and pull it through both stitches. Slip both stitches off the needle. One stitch has been decreased.

1

2

1

2

3

Working a basic left-slanting decrease

Slip 1, knit 1, pass slip stitch over is a left-slanting decrease that mirrors the slant of the knit 2 together decrease, shown left, when worked on a right-side row. For a neat finish when shaping, work a right-slanting decrease near the beginning of the row and a left-slanting decrease near the end.

1 Work to the point indicated in the pattern. Slip the next stitch from the left needle knitwise onto the right needle. Knit the next stitch in the usual way.

2 Insert the tip of the left needle into the front of the slipped stitch and lift the slipped stitch over the knit stitch and off the right needle. One stitch has been decreased.

1

2

PRESSING AND BLOCKING

Press knitting lightly on the wrong side, setting your iron temperature according to the information given on the ball band of your yarn. Avoid pressing synthetic yarns as they will become limp and lifeless—or melt—with too much heat. Press ribbed items very lightly as they may flatten and lose their stretch.

Blocking (shown below) involves pinning the knit fabric to the correct size, then either steaming it with an iron or moistening it with cold water depending on the fiber content of your yarn. Pin your finished item to the correct size on a flat surface, such as your ironing board or a special blocking board using rust-proof pins. It's a good idea to block gauge swatches (page 18) before measuring them.

1

1 To block woolen yarns with steam, hold a steam iron set at the correct temperature for the yarn about $3/4$ in. (2 cm) above the surface of the knitting and allow the steam to penetrate for several seconds without allowing the iron to come into contact with the fabric. Lay the board flat and allow to dry before removing the pins.

2 To block synthetic and wool/synthetic blend yarns, pin as above, then use a spray bottle to mist the item with clean, cold water until it is evenly moist all over, but not saturated. Pat with your hand to help the moisture penetrate more easily. Lay the board flat and allow to dry before removing the pins.

2

SEAMS

There are several methods of joining pieces of knitting. The methods shown below are both good for assembling garments. Use the same yarn for both knitting and seams, unless your yarn is very thick or textured, in which case use a finer yarn of matching color. A backstitch seam is durable and has little stretch, so use this method for seaming bags. An overcast seam has more stretch and works best for seaming hats. Use either method for seaming mittens and capelets.

Overcast seam

1 Pin the right sides together, inserting the pins parallel to and a few stitches away from the edge. Secure the yarn by taking a few stitches over the top of the seam.

2 With your index finger between the layers, insert the needle from back to front through both layers as close to the edge as you can. Repeat along the seam.

Backstitch seam

1 Place the edges to be joined together with the right sides of the knitting facing each other and pin them together, inserting the pins at right angles to the edge. Thread the yarn into a yarn needle and secure the yarn at the right edge of the seam by working 2 or 3 small stitches around the 2 edges ending with the yarn in front.

2 Insert the needle into the knitting just behind the end of the previous stitch, bringing the point through a short distance in front to make the first back stitch.

3 Put the needle back into the knitting where the previous stitch ended and make another stitch the same length as before. Repeat Step 3 along the seam, taking care not to pull the stitches too tightly.

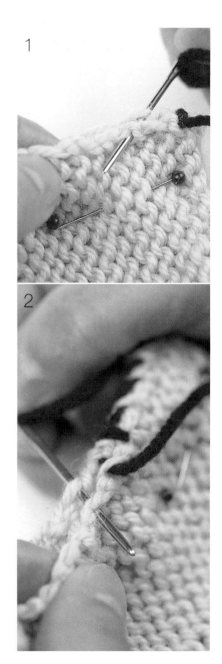

Basic Patterns

This section contains basic patterns for a knitted bag, scarf, pair of mittens, hat, and capelet. The best starting projects for a beginner are the garter stitch scarf on this page and the rib hat on page 27.

THE BASIC BAG—BUTTONHOLE BAG

YOU WILL NEED

2 balls of pure wool chunky yarn with approx 100 yds (92 m) per 100 g ball

Pair of size 10 (6 mm) knitting needles or size needed to achieve gauge

Yarn needle

FINISHED SIZE

Bag measures 9 $^1/_2$ in. (14 cm) deep and 11 $^1/_2$ in. (29 cm) wide.

GAUGE

15 stitches and 19 rows to 4 in. (10 cm) over measured over stockinette stitch

KNITTING THE BAG FRONT

CO 42 sts.
ROW 1: (RS) Knit.
ROW 2: K1, P to last st, K1.
Rep Rows 1 and 2 until 42 rows are worked, ending with a WS row.

Make buttonhole

BUTTONHOLE ROW: (RS) K12, bring yarn to front, slip next stitch purlwise, take yarn to back, * slip next stitch on left needle, pass first slipped stitch over it and off right needle; rep from * 17 times more (18 sts bound off). Slip last BO stitch on right needle to left needle and turn work. CO 19 sts and turn work again. With yarn at back, slip first stitch from left needle onto right needle, pass first CO stitch over it and off needle, knit remaining 11 sts. (42 sts)

Shape handle

ROW 1: (WS) K1, P to last st, K1.
ROW 2: Knit.
Rep Rows 1 and 2 once, then rep Row 1 once more. BO all stitches.

KNITTING THE BAG BACK

Work as for front.

FINISHING THE BAG

Press pieces lightly on wrong side. Weave in yarn ends on wrong side using yarn needle. Place pieces together with right sides facing and pin around edges. Using same yarn in yarn needle, backstitch down one side, across bottom and up second side. Turn bag to right side.

THE BASIC SCARF

YOU WILL NEED

2 balls of pure wool chunky yarn with approx 100 yds (92 m) per 100 g ball

Pair of size 10 $^1/_2$ (6.5 mm) knitting needles or size needed to achieve gauge

Yarn needle

FINISHED SIZE

Scarf measures 5 $^1/_2$ in. (14 cm) wide and 48 in. (122 cm) long.

GAUGE

15 stitches and 26 rows to 4 in. (10 cm) measured over garter stitch.

KNITTING THE SCARF

CO 22 sts.
ROW 1: (WS) Knit to end.
ROW 2: (RS) Knit to end.
Using garter stitch throughout (knit every row), work until scarf is approx 48 in. (122 cm) long, ending with a RS row.
NEXT ROW: (WS) BO all stitches.

FINISHING THE SCARF

Weave in yarn ends on wrong side using yarn needle.

THE BASIC MITTENS

YOU WILL NEED

2 [2, 2] balls of pure wool chunky yarn with approx 100 yds (92 m) per 100 g ball

Pair of size 8 (5 mm) and size 9 (5.5 mm) knitting needles or sizes needed to achieve gauge

Yarn needle

SIZES

To fit women's sizes Small, Medium, Large (instructions for Medium and Large sizes are given in square brackets).

SPECIAL ABBREVIATION

M1 = make an extra stitch (see Working a make-one increase, page 21)

GAUGE

15 stitches and 20 rows to 4 in. (10 cm) measured over stockinette stitch using size 9 (5.5 mm) needles.

KNITTING THE RIGHT MITTEN

Using size 8 (5 mm) needles, CO 29 [33, 37] sts.

ROW 1: (RS) K1, * P1, K1; rep from * to end.
ROW 2: * P1, K1; rep from * to last st, P1.
Rep Rows 1 and 2 for 2 [2, 2¹/₂] in. (5 [5, 6] cm), ending with a RS row.
NEXT ROW: Rib 6 sts, M1, (rib 4 [5, 6] sts, M1) 4 times, rib 7 sts. (34 [38, 42] sts)
Change to size 9 (5.5 mm) needles and stockinette stitch (RS rows knit, WS rows purl).
Beg with a knit row, work 4 [4, 6] rows of St st. **

Shape thumb gusset

ROW 1: (RS) K17 [19, 21], M1, K3, M1, K to end. (36 [40, 44] sts)
Work 3 rows of St st without shaping.
ROW 5: K17 [19, 21], M1, K5, M1, K to end. (38 [42, 46] sts)
ROW 6 and every alt row: Purl.
ROW 7: K17 [19, 21], M1, K7, M1, K to end. (40 [44, 48] sts)
Cont as set, inc 2 sts on every foll alt row until there are 44 [48, 52] sts on the needle.
NEXT ROW: Purl.

Divide for thumb

NEXT ROW: (RS) K30 [32, 34], turn.
*** NEXT ROW: P11 [13, 13], turn.
Working on these 11 [13, 13] sts only, work 8 [10, 12] rows without shaping.
NEXT ROW: K1, * K2tog; rep from * to end. (6 [7, 7] sts)
Break off yarn, leaving long tail of about 12 in. (30 cm). Thread end into yarn needle and slide needle through remaining stitches on knitting needle. Pull yarn gently to gather stitches and slip off knitting needle.
With RS facing, rejoin yarn at base of thumb and knit to end of row. (33 [35, 39] sts)
Work 13 [15, 17] rows without shaping.

Shape top

ROW 1: (RS) K1, (sl 1, K1, psso, K11 [12, 14], K2tog, K1) twice. (29 [31, 35] sts)
ROW 2 and every alt row: Purl.
ROW 3: K1, (sl 1, K1, psso, K9 [10, 12] K2tog, K1) twice.
Cont as set, dec 4 sts on every foll alt row until there are 21 [23, 23] sts on needle, ending with a WS row.
BO all stitches.

KNITTING THE LEFT MITTEN

Work as given for right mitten up to **.

Shape thumb gusset

ROW 1: (RS) K14 [16, 18], M1, K3, M1, K to end. (36 [40, 44] sts)
Work 3 rows of St st without shaping.
ROW 5: K14 [16, 18], M1, K5, M1, K to end. (38 [42, 46] sts)
ROW 6 and every alt row: Purl.
ROW 7: K14 [16, 18], M1, K7, M1, K to end. (40 [44, 48] sts)
Cont as set, inc 2 sts on every foll alt row until there are 44 [48, 52] sts on the needle.
NEXT ROW: Purl.

Divide for thumb

NEXT ROW: (RS) K27 [29, 31], turn.
Work as given for right mitten from ***.

FINISHING THE MITTENS

Press mittens lightly on wrong side. Using long yarn tail yarn in yarn needle, join thumb seam using backstitch seam or overcast seam. Weave in yarn ends on wrong side with yarn needle. With matching yarn in yarn needle, join remaining seams using either backstitch seam or overcast seam.

THE BASIC HAT

YOU WILL NEED

1 ball of pure wool chunky yarn with approx 100 yds (92 m) per 100 g ball

Pair of size 10 (6 mm) and size 10 ^{1}/$_{2}$ (7 mm) knitting needles or sizes needed to achieve gauge

Yarn needle

FINISHED SIZE

Hat measures 8 in. (20 cm) deep and will fit average adult head.

GAUGE

16 stitches and 18 rows measured over double rib, slightly stretched widthwise, using size 10 (6 mm) needles.

KNITTING THE HAT

Using size 10 ^{1}/$_{2}$ (7 mm) needles, CO 72 sts.
Change to size 10 (6 mm) needles.
ROW 1: (RS) * K2, P2; rep from * to end.
Rep Row 1 until you have worked 33 rows. (72 sts)

Shape hat crown

ROW 1: (WS) * K2 tog, P2; rep from * to end. (54 sts)
ROW 2: * K2 tog, P1; rep from * to end. (36 sts)

ROWS 3 and 4: * K1, P1; rep from * to end.
ROW 5: * K2 tog; rep from * to end. (18 sts)
ROW 6: * K2 tog; rep from * to end. (9 sts)

FINISHING THE HAT

Break off yarn, leaving a long tail of about 15 in. (38 cm). Thread end into yarn needle and slot needle through remaining stitches on knitting needle. Pull yarn gently to gather stitches and slip off knitting needle. Press hat lightly on wrong side. Using long yarn tail yarn in yarn needle, join with overcast seam. Weave in yarn end on wrong side.

THE BASIC CAPELET

YOU WILL NEED

2 100 g of pure wool Icelandic Lopi yarn with approx 109 yds (100 m) per 100 g ball

Pair of size 10 ^{1}/$_{2}$ (6.5 mm) knitting needles or size needed to achieve gauge

Yarn needle

FINISHED SIZE

Capelet measures 7 in. (18 cm) deep and 48 in. (122 cm) in circumference along lower edge from front to back. Ties are 15 in. (38 cm) long.

GAUGE

13 stitches and 17 rows to 4 in. (10 cm) measured over stockinette stitch.

KNITTING THE PANELS (make two; each panel is a front and back half)

CO 75 sts and knit 5 rows.

Shape front and back edges

ROW 6: (RS) K2, sl 1, K1, psso, K67, K2tog, K2. (73 sts)
ROWS 7, 9, 11, 13, 15 and 17: K1, P to last st, K1.

ROW 8: K2, sl 1, K1, psso, K65, K2tog, K2. (71 sts)
ROW 10: K2, sl 1, K1, psso, K63, K2tog, K2. (69 sts)
ROW 12: K2, sl 1, K1, psso, K61, K2tog, K2. (67 sts)
ROW 14: K2, sl 1, K1, psso, K59, K2tog, K2. (65 sts)
ROW 16: K2, sl 1, K1, psso, K57, K2tog, K2. (63 sts)
ROW 18: K2, sl 1, K1, psso, K55, K2tog, K2. (61 sts)
ROW 19: K1, P to last st, K1.

Shape shoulder

ROW 1: (RS) K2, sl 1, K1, psso, K23, K2tog, K3, sl 1, K1, psso, K23, K2tog, K2. (57 sts)
ROWS 2, 4, 6 and 8: K1, P to last st, K1.
ROW 3: K2, sl 1, K1, psso, K21, K2tog, K3, sl 1, K1, psso, K21, K2tog, K2. (53 sts)
ROW 5: K2, sl 1, K1, psso, K19, K2tog, K3, sl 1, K1, psso, K19, K2tog, K2. (49 sts)
ROW 7: K2, sl 1, K1, psso, K17, K2tog, K3, sl 1, K1, psso, K17, K2tog, K2. (45 sts)
ROW 9: K2, sl 1, K1, psso, K15, K2tog,

K3, sl 1, K1, psso, K15, K2tog, K2. (41 sts)
ROWS 10 to 12: Knit. BO all stitches.

KNITTING THE TIES (make two)

CO 45 sts. Knit 2 rows. BO all stitches.

FINISHING THE CAPELET

Press pieces lightly on wrong side. Weave in yarn ends on wrong side using yarn needle. Pin 2 main pieces together with right sides facing and 2 outside edges aligning to form seam down center back. Using same yarn in yarn needle, backstitch edges together. Pin short edge of tie to wrong side of each front edge at neckline and stitch securely to capelet.

chapter 2
edgings and trimmings

Delightfully fluffy **pompoms**, **knotted fringes**, and embroidered **appliqué** shapes are just some of the edgings and trimmings used in this chapter to transform our **five basic accessories**. Many of the projects have a **variation** that shows how the main technique can be adapted to another item. Feel free to alter the colors and designs to suit your own style and your wardrobe, or to combine the ideas here with those from other chapters. Why not add beads to the **picot hem** of the Julia mittens on page 41, for example?

playful

scarf with pompoms

Pompoms are fun decorations to stitch to each corner of a plain garter stitch scarf. The secret to making a delightfully fluffy pompom is to use plenty of yarn, which can be all of one color or a combination of several colors and types of yarn to give a multicolored effect.

Prefer the bag? see page 25 for the basic pattern

YOU WILL NEED

- 4 balls of pure wool double knitting yarn with approx 131 yds (120 m) per 50 g ball
- Leftovers of the same yarn in 2 or 3 contrasting colors
- Pair of size 10$\frac{1}{2}$ (6.5 mm) knitting needles or size needed to achieve gauge
- Pompom maker or stiff cardboard, outer ring 2$\frac{1}{4}$ in. (5.5 cm) diameter
- Yarn needle

NOTE

Yarn is used double throughout. You can buy sets of adjustable plastic pompom rings or simply cut two identical doughnut shapes from sturdy cardboard. When cutting your own shapes, make the center ring about one quarter of the diameter of the outer ring.

FINISHED SIZE

Scarf measures 6 in. (15 cm) wide and 48 in. (122 cm) long

GAUGE

15 stitches and 26 rows to 4 in. (10 cm) measured over garter stitch.

KNITTING THE SCARF

Using two strands of yarn, knit and finish the scarf following the basic pattern on page 25.

MAKING THE POMPOMS

1 Place 2 pompom rings (or cardboard circles) back to back. Thread several strands of yarn in yarn needle. Wind yarn around rings, adding lengths of yarn until center space is tightly filled.

2 Using sharp scissors, carefully cut through yarn strands, easing scissor points between pompom rings.

3 Ease rings apart and tie a length of matching yarn firmly around strands in middle of rings.

4 Pull rings apart and ease them off yarn strands. Trim off uneven pieces of yarn for a neat finish. Leave yarn ties untrimmed.

5 To attach pompoms to scarf, thread ends of yarn ties in yarn needle and stitch pompom securely in place at each corner.

pompom bag

Decorate each side of the handle of a felted Buttonhole Bag with a brightly colored pompom made with three contrasting yarns. Thread the long ends of the ties in a yarn needle and stitch the pompoms in place. (See pages 112 and 113 for more on felting.)

weekend

scarf with fringe

A simple fringe makes a great finishing touch for a scarf knit in double rib. You can use the same yarn or add a fringe in another color or texture.

YOU WILL NEED

- 3 balls of pure wool chunky yarn with 87 yds (80 m) per 100 g
- Pair of size 10½ (6.5 mm) knitting needles or size needed to achieve gauge
- Stiff cardboard
- Large crochet hook
- Yarn needle

FINISHED SIZE

Scarf measures 6 in. (15 cm) wide and 55 in. (140 cm) long, not including the fringe.

GAUGE

13 stitches and 18 rows to 4 in. (10 cm) measured over double rib.

KNITTING THE SCARF

CO 22 sts following the basic Scarf pattern on page 25.

ROW 1: (RS) * K2, P2; rep from * to last 2 sts, K2.

ROW 2: * P2, K2; rep from * to last 2 sts, P2.

Rep Rows 1 and 2 until scarf measures approximately 55 in. (140 cm) long. BO.

FINISHING THE SCARF

Finish the scarf as described in the basic pattern on page 25.

Prefer the lattice scarf? **see page 25 for basic pattern**

1

MAKING THE FRINGE

1 Decide how long finished fringe will be and cut a rectangle of stiff cardboard to same length plus 1 in. (2.5 cm). Wind yarn evenly around cardboard and cut along bottom edge to make strands.

2 Insert large crochet hook from back to front of knitted edge of scarf. Gather 4 strands into group, fold in half and loop fold over hook.

3 Carefully pull hook and folded strands of yarn through to wrong side of knitting to make loop.

4 Loop crochet hook around cut ends of yarn group and pull gently through the loop to complete tassel. Repeat at regularly-spaced intervals along edge. Neaten ends by trimming any long strands.

2

3

4

lattice scarf

Make a knotted, lattice fringe for a more elaborate finish. Cut the strands twice as long as for a simple fringe and knot into the edge, spacing the tassels further apart. Take half the strands from one group and half the strands from an adjacent group and knot them together with an overhand knot. Repeat along the edge.

sporty

scarf with blanket-stitch edging

A quick and easy embroidery edge turns a plain stockinette stitch scarf into a casual yet stylish accessory. Choosing a strong color contrast for the stitching will guarantee your handiwork stands out!

YOU WILL NEED

- 2 balls of pure wool chunky yarn with approx 100 yds (92 m) per 100 g ball
- Leftovers of the same yarn in a contrasting color
- Pair of size 10¹/₂ (6.5 mm) knitting needles or size needed to achieve gauge
- Yarn needle

FINISHED SIZE

Scarf measures 6 in. (15 cm) wide and 80 in. (203 cm) long.

GAUGE

14 stitches and 18 rows to 4 in. (10 cm) over stockinette stitch.

KNITTING THE SCARF

CO 22 sts following the basic pattern on page 25.

ROW 1: (RS) Knit.

ROW 2: K1, P to last st, K1.

Rep Rows 1 and 2 until the scarf is approximately 80 in. (203 cm) long, ending with a WS row. BO.

Weave in the yarn ends and press lightly on the wrong side.

WORKING THE BLANKET-STITCH EDGING

1 Thread contrasting yarn in yarn needle. Begin stitching at center of 1 long side. Insert needle into knitting about 3 or 4 stitches from edge and leave tail of yarn on surface. Bring needle back through knitting close to edge so it is ready to begin stitching. Tail will be secured after length of yarn has been used.

2 Take needle through knitting from front to back about $^3/_4$ in. (1.5 cm) from edge and same distance to right from point where yarn emerged along edge. Take working thread under point of needle.

3 Carefully pull needle and yarn through to complete first blanket stitch. Repeat along edge, making evenly spaced stitches, until last stitch is worked about $^3/_4$ in. (1.5 cm) from corner.

4 To make a neat corner, work 1 blanket stitch diagonally across corner so it shares same hole as previous stitch. To complete corner, make another blanket stitch to share same hole, working it along adjacent side of scarf.

5 To finish off yarn ends, take them through to wrong side and weave them in as neatly as possible close to edge of knitting, then trim.

Tip

Choose a novelty yarn to work the blanket stitches. Ribbon and tape yarns work well for embroidery, but avoid eyelash yarns and those that are heavily textured.

curly

bag with curly fringe

Knitted fringes are fun to
work, and this one creates
wonderful corkscrew curls.
Use a length of matching
fringe to decorate the lower
edge of a plain buttonhole
bag or a garter stitch scarf.

YOU WILL NEED

- 2 balls of pure wool chunky yarn with
  approx 100 yds (92 m) per 100 g ball
- Pair of size 9 (5.5 mm) and size 10
  (6 mm) knitting needles or size needed
  to achieve gauge
- Sewing thread and sewing needle
- Yarn needle

FINISHED SIZE

Bag measures 14 in. (36 cm) deep,
including fringe, and 11½ in. (29 cm)
wide.

GAUGE

15 stitches and 19 rows to 4 in. (10 cm)
over stockinette stitch using size 10
(6 mm) needles.

KNITTING THE BAG

Knit the back and front of the bag with the
size 10 (6 mm) needles following the
basic pattern on page 25.

FRINGE PATTERN

Using size 9 (5.5 mm) needles, CO 20
sts.
ROW 1: (RS) BO 15 sts, K4.
ROW 2: K5.
ROW 3: CO 15 sts.
Rep Rows 1 to 3 for length required,
ending with a Row 1. BO.

Prefer the scarf? **see page 25 for the basic pattern**

KNITTING THE FRINGE

1 Cast on 20 stitches. Bind off 15 stitches to leave 4 stitches on left needle and 1 stitch on right needle.

2 Knit remaining 4 stitches. There are now 5 stitches on right needle. Turn work and knit 5 stitches.

3 Turn work and cast on 15 stitches. There are now 20 stitches on needle.

4 Repeat Steps 1 to 3 to make strip of fringe long enough to fit across bottom of bag. End by binding off 15 stitches as if you were working Row 1 of pattern. Bind off remaining stitches.

5 Position fringe on right side of bag front with right sides facing, aligning lower edge of bag with top edge of fringe. Baste in place with sewing thread.

FINISHING THE BAG

Finish the bag as described in the basic pattern, making sure you place the right sides of both front and back pieces together so the fringe is sandwiched between them.

1

2

3

4

5

kinky scarf

Liven up the basic Scarf by knitting two short lengths of curly fringe and stitching them across each end. You can use matching yarn as shown, or choose one of contrasting weight and texture.

violet

felted bag with fabric binding

Add a touch of color and pattern to a plain felted bag by binding the top edge with a bias strip of printed cotton fabric.

YOU WILL NEED

- 2 balls of pure wool Icelandic Lopi yarn with approx 109 yds (100 m) per 100 g ball
- Pair of size 10½ (7.5 mm) knitting needles or size needed to achieve gauge
- Scraps of printed cotton fabric to complement yarn
- Matching sewing thread and sewing needle
- Yarn needle

FINISHED SIZE

Bag is 9 in. (23 cm) deep and 12 in. (30 cm) wide after felting.

GAUGE

Working to an exact gauge is not necessary when making a felted bag. Knit a gauge swatch using the stated needles and machine wash it in hot water. The knit fabric should feel thick and substantial and have lost most of the stitch definition, but still be pliable. You may need to knit several swatches using different needle sizes to get a felted fabric that feels right. There's more information about felting on pages 112 and 113.

KNITTING THE BAG

Knit the bag front following the basic pattern on page 25, but do not bind off.

NEXT ROW: (RS) K1, P to last st, K1.

NEXT ROW: Knit. BO. Repeat for bag back.

FINISHING THE BAG

Finish the bag as described in the basic pattern, omitting pressing. Machine wash in hot water and spin dry. Pull the bag gently into shape and lay flat until completely dry.

Prefer the scarf? **see page 25 for the basic pattern**

APPLYING THE BINDING

1 Fold cotton fabric across diagonal and press fold. Mark several 1¹/₂ in. (4 cm) strips across fabric following line of fold. Cut along lines through both layers of fabric.

2 Place ends of 2 strips with right sides together and back stitch across, close to edge. Join several strips in same way to make length that will go around top of bag, plus overlap of about 1 in. (2.5 cm). Press strip, pressing seams open.

3 Cut ends of strip square. Fold strip in half lengthwise with wrong sides together and press fold. To finish making binding, turn a narrow hem along both long edges and baste to secure.

4 Turning under raw edges at each end of binding, pin binding around top of bag to enclose bag edge, overlapping ends of strip by about ¹/₂ in. (1 cm). Stitch binding in place on right side of bag with small stitches and matching thread, then repeat on wrong side. Remove basting.

bound scarf

A fabric binding makes a pretty edge on the basic Scarf. Make the binding as narrow or as wide as you like.

julia

mittens with picot hem

Instead of knitting an ordinary single or double rib cuff on your winter mittens, add a pretty picot hem. The decoration is easy to work and adds a dressy look to plain mittens.

WORKING THE PICOT HEM

1 Begin picot row by knitting first 2 stitches with size 8 (5 mm) needles. Bring yarn forward between needles, insert right needle into both of next 2 stitches knitwise, wrap yarn around needle and knit 2 stitches together. Continue along row alternating working 1 yarn over with knitting 2 stitches together.

2 Change to size 9 (5.5 mm) needles and work next row, purling knit stitches and yarn overs made on previous row.

3 With right sides together, sew mitten seams. Fold hem to wrong side so fold runs across picot row and pin in place, inserting pins at right angles to hem.

4 Using same yarn, carefully stitch hem to mitten. Turn mitten to right side and lightly press hem with a warm iron.

YOU WILL NEED

- 2 [2, 2] balls of pure wool chunky yarn with approx 100 yds (92 m) per 100 g ball
- Pair of size 8 (5 mm) and size 9 (5.5 mm) knitting needles or size needed to achieve gauge
- Yarn needle

FINISHED SIZES

To fit women's sizes Small, Medium, Large (instructions for Medium and Large sizes are given in square brackets).

GAUGE

15 stitches and 20 rows to 4 in. (10 cm) over stockinette stitch using size 9 (5.5 mm) needles.

KNITTING THE MITTENS

Using size 8 (5 mm) needles, CO 34 [38, 42] sts.

ROWS 1 and 3: (RS) Knit.

ROWS 2 and 4: Purl.

ROW 5: (RS, picot row) K2, * YO, K2tog; rep from * to end.

Change to size 9 (5.5 mm) needles.

Beg with a purl (WS) row, work 9 [9, 11] rows in St st.

Change to following the basic pattern on page 26, working from "Shape thumb gusset" to end.

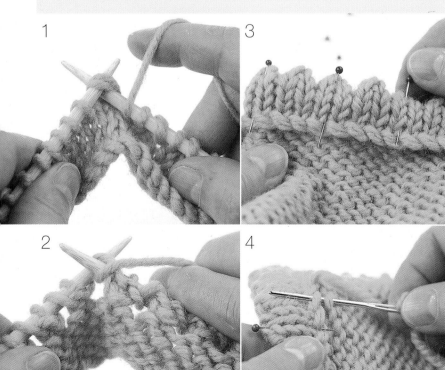

meadow

bag with felt appliqué flowers

Stitching bold felt shapes onto a plain stockinette stitch bag is a quick way to turn it into something special. If you don't want to stitch the shapes, use fabric glue or fusible bonding web to secure them.

YOU WILL NEED

- 2 balls of pure wool chunky yarn with approx 100 yds (92 m) per 100 g ball
- Pair of size 10 (6 mm) knitting needles or size needed to achieve gauge
- Thin cardboard
- Scraps of yellow and red felt
- Yellow and green embroidery floss
- Crewel embroidery needle
- Yarn needle

FINISHED SIZE

Bag measures $9\frac{1}{2}$ in. (24 cm) deep and $11\frac{1}{2}$ in. (29 cm) wide.

GAUGE

15 stitches and 19 rows to 4 in. (10 cm) over stockinette stitch.

KNITTING THE BAG

Knit the back and front of the bag following the basic pattern on page 25.

Prefer the mittens? **see page 26 for the basic pattern**

WORKING THE APPLIQUE

1 Using photograph as guide to shape, draw outline of simple flower on piece of cardboard. Cut out flower to make template. Make template for flower center in same way by drawing around a coin or bottle top.

2 Lay flower template on yellow felt and draw around it with fine-point felt pen. Repeat twice more. Do same with flower center template on red felt. Using sharp pair of scissors, cut out flowers and centers.

3 Position flowers in row along base of bag and pin in place. Using 3 strands of yellow embroidery floss, stitch flowers onto knitting with blanket stitch (page 115).

4 Pin center on each flower. Using 3 strands of green embroidery floss, stitch flower centers with straight stitches around edge of felt.

dotty mittens

Decorate a pair of basic Mittens with colorful polka dots embroidered with straight stitches worked in a contrasting color of embroidery floss.

paris

rib hat with French knit trim

You may remember making lengths of French (or spool) knitting when you were a child. Traditionally, the circular knitted cord was worked over four small nails attached to a wooden spool, but today you can buy a ready-made knitting spool, which is easier to use.

YOU WILL NEED

- 1 ball of pure wool chunky yarn with approx 100 yds (92 m) per 100 g
- Small amounts of double knitting yarn in a contrasting color
- Pair of size 10 (6 mm) and size 10$\frac{1}{2}$ (7 mm) knitting needles or size needed to achieve gauge
- Knitting nancy (or knitting spool)
- Yarn needle

FINISHED SIZE

Hat measures 8 in. (20 cm) deep and 18 in. (46 cm) in circumference.

GAUGE

16 stitches and 18 rows to 4 in. (10 cm) measured over double rib, slightly stretched widthwise, using size 10 (6 mm) needles.

KNITTING THE HAT

Knit the hat following the basic pattern on page 27.

Prefer the scarf? **see page 25 for basic pattern**

MAKING THE CORD

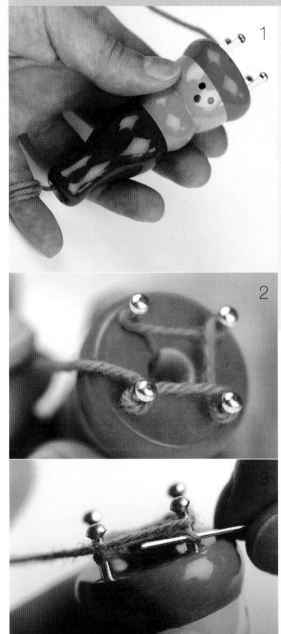

1 Thread end of yarn through knitting nancy until it emerges from bottom. Wind yarn end around little finger to keep it taut and stop it from slipping.

2 Keeping yarn end tensioned, wrap yarn coming from ball around each nail counter-clockwise and pull taut.

3 Lay yarn over first wrap on nail. Lift wrap over yarn and off nail using yarn needle. Work each stitch in this way, pulling yarn at bottom of nancy to keep it tensioned, until cord is 16 in. (40 cm) long.

4 To bind off, move last knitted stitch to nail at its left. Lift bottom stitch over top stitch. Repeat until 1 stitch remains, then fasten off yarn.

FINISHING THE HAT

Finish the hat as described in the basic pattern on page 27. Weave in the yarn ends of the cord, then tie a knot at each end. Using the photograph as a guide, wind the cord to make a pleasing shape and pin in place. Stitch to the hat using the cord yarn.

loopy scarf

To jazz up the basic Scarf, add several loops of contrasting French knit cord along the ends. Stitch each loop securely in place using matching yarn.

jaunty

rib hat with turn-back cuff

The classic ribbed hat looks good when a deep, turn-back cuff is added. Knit the hat in single or double rib using a solid yarn color or vary the effect by choosing a funky, variegated yarn.

MAKING THE CUFF AND FINISHING THE HAT

YOU WILL NEED

- 1 ball of pure wool chunky yarn with approx 100 yds (92 m) per 100 g
- Pair of size 10 (6 mm) and size 10½ (6.5 mm) knitting needles or size needed to achieve gauge
- Stitch markers or scraps of contrasting yarn
- Yarn needle

FINISHED SIZE

Hat measures 8 in. (20 cm) deep and 18 in. (46 cm) in circumference. Cuff is 3 in. (8 cm) deep.

GAUGE

16 stitches and 18 rows to 4 in. (10 cm) measured over single rib, slightly stretched widthwise, using size 10 (6 mm) needles.

KNITTING THE CUFF AND HAT

CO 72 sts with size 10½ (6.5 mm) needles following the basic pattern on page 27.

ROW 1: (RS of cuff, WS of hat) * K1, P1; rep from * to end.

Rep Row 1 until you have worked 13 more rows, ending with a WS row. (72 sts)

Mark each end of row with a stitch marker or piece of spare yarn.

Change to size 10 (6 mm) needles.

Cont to work even in single rib until you have worked 29 more rows, ending with a RS row. (72 sts)

SHAPE CROWN OF HAT

ROW 1: (WS) K1, * K2 tog, P1, K1; rep from * to last 3 sts, K2tog, P1. (54 sts)

ROW 2: * K1, K2 tog; rep from * to end. (36 sts)

ROWS 3 and 4: * P1, K1; rep from * to end.

ROW 5: * P2 tog; rep from * to end. (18 sts)

ROW 6: * K2 tog; rep from * to end. (9 sts)

Break off yarn, leaving tail of about 8 in. (20 cm). Thread end into yarn needle and slide needle through remaining stitches on knitting needle. Pull yarn gently to gather stitches and slip off knitting needle. Darn in yarn end. Finish hat as shown at right.

1 Cast on required number of stitches with size 10½ (6.5 mm) needles, leaving 15 in. (38 cm) long tail of yarn at beginning. Tail will be used to sew cuff.

2 Work 14 rows of single rib as instructed, ending with wrong side row. With right side of work facing you, mark each end of Row 14 with stitch marker.

3 If you don't have stitch markers handy, cut two 8 in (20 cm) lengths of contrasting yarn. Use yarn needle to insert length of contrasting yarn at each end of row, then knot yarn ends securely.

4 Follow pattern instructions and complete hat. With wrong sides of cuff facing, use yarn tail to stitch cuff seam about ½ in. (1 cm) beyond markers. With wrong sides of hat facing, complete hat seam.

5 Turn cuff to right side along Row 14. Working from right side of cuff, catch edge of cuff to hat with a few stitches worked into seam.

swinger

rib hat with tassel

One huge, generous tassel decorates this double rib hat. Making tassels is a great way to use up odd lengths of yarn from your stash. Mini tassels look cute added to mittens.

YOU WILL NEED:

- 1 ball of pure wool chunky yarn with approx 100 yds (92 m) per 100 g
- Small amounts of 3 coordinating chunky yarns
- Pair of size 10 (6 mm) and size 10¹/₂ (7 mm) knitting needles or size needed to achieve gauge
- Stiff cardboard
- Yarn needle

FINISHED SIZE

Hat measures 8 in. (20 cm) deep and 18 in. (46 cm) in circumference. Tassel measures 6 in. (15 cm) long.

GAUGE

16 stitches and 18 rows to 4 in. (10 cm) measured over double rib, slightly stretched widthwise, using size 10 (6 mm) needles.

KNITTING THE HAT

Knit and finish the hat following the basic pattern on page 27.

Prefer the mittens? **see page 26 for the basic pattern**

MAKING THE TASSEL

1 Decide how long you want finished tassel to be and cut rectangle of stiff cardboard to same length plus 1 in. (2.5 cm). Using all 4 colors together, wind yarn evenly around card 5 or 6 times, starting and ending along bottom edge of card.

2 Pass short length of main yarn under strands at top of card and knot ends tightly together. Cut strands along bottom edge of card where you began winding.

3 Holding strands together in group close to knot, wrap length of main yarn tightly around top of strands about ½ in. (1 cm) from knot.

4 Secure end of yarn by threading it in yarn needle and taking it down through center of wraps.

5 Trim ends of tassel evenly. Thread length of yarn knotted around top of tassel into yarn needle, pull through top of hat to wrong side and secure with several stitches

1

2

3

4

5

tasseled mittens

For a fun finish, add several tiny matching tassels to the cuff edge of a pair of basic Mittens. These tassels are made from 12 strands of chunky yarn.

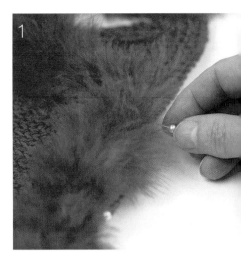

swansdown

capelet with marabou trim

Wear this delightfully feminine capelet over a floaty summer dress and fasten it with ribbon ties (see Bluebell, page 74) or use a glamorous, sparkly pin or clasp.

YOU WILL NEED

- 3 balls of pure wool double knitting yarn with approx 131 yds (120 m) per 50 g ball
- Pair of size 10 (6 mm) and size 10½ (6.5 mm) knitting needles or size needed to achieve gauge
- 3 yds (2.75 m) of marabou trim
- Sewing thread to match yarn
- Sewing needle
- Yarn needle

NOTE

Yarn is used double throughout.

FINISHED SIZE

Capelet measures 6 in. (15 cm) deep and 42 in. (107 cm) in circumference along lower edge from front to back.

GAUGE

15 stitches and 20 rows to 4 in. (10 cm) measured over stockinette stitch using size 10 (6 mm) needles.

KNITTING THE CAPELET

Using two strands of yarn, knit and finish the capelet following the basic pattern on page 27, omitting the ties.

Prefer the bag? see page 25 for the basic pattern

APPLYING MARABOU TRIM

1 Pin marabou trim around capelet on right side, starting at center back seam of lower edge and inserting pins at right angles to edge of knitting.

2 At corner, allow for a little extra trim to go around angle, making sure trim lies flat in wear.

3 Continue pinning trim around capelet in same way until you reach starting point. Overlap ends of trim by about ³⁄₄ in. (2 cm).

4 Stitch trim in place by sewing core of it carefully to right side of knitting using sewing thread that matches yarn color. Take stitches through trim from back of knitting at right angles to core, pulling feathers free when making each stitch. Secure thread ends neatly on wrong side.

fluffy bag

Marabou trim adds a touch of glamour to a plain gray Buttonhole Bag. Position the marabou along the bottom edge, as shown, or take it up the sides as well for a bolder effect.

chapter 3
fastenings and handles

Chapter 3 contains over a dozen fabulous ideas for using a wide range of both **handmade** and store-bought handles and fastenings. Knitted, tied ends transform a plain scarf into an Octopus scarf that you might like to combine with the bag with **knotted** handles. Felted **drawstring** handles make a fun closure for a chunky felted bag. Divine, **sparkly buttons** make pretty fastenings for our Loopy mittens, while the basic capelet is turned into an elegant Bluebell wrap on page 74 thanks to the addition of lengths of **satin ribbon**.

tuck

scarf with slit closure

This project makes use of two colors of closely toned yarn, but there's no reason why you shouldn't combine two strongly contrasting colors for a dynamic effect. To wear the scarf, tuck the plain end through the slit.

YOU WILL NEED

- 4 balls of pure wool double knitting yarn with approx 131 yds (120 m) per 50 g ball; 2 balls in main color and 2 balls in contrast color
- Pair of size 9 (5.5 mm) knitting needles or size needed to achieve gauge
- 2 stitch holders
- Yarn needle

NOTE

One strand of main yarn and one strand of contrast yarn are used together throughout.

FINISHED SIZE

Scarf measures 5$\frac{1}{2}$ in. (14 cm) wide and 39 in. (100 cm) long.

GAUGE

17 stitches and 26 rows to 4 in. (10 cm) measured over garter stitch.

KNITTING THE SCARF

Holding both yarns together, CO 22 sts with size 9 (5.5 mm) needles following the basic pattern on page 25.

Work in garter stitch for 6 in. (15 cm), ending with a WS row.

* DIVIDE FOR SLIT OPENING

NEXT ROW: K11, slip rem 11 sts onto stitch holder, turn.

Work in garter stitch on these 11 sts for 4 in. (10 cm), ending with a WS row. Put these 11 sts onto second stitch holder and break yarn, leaving tail to weave in.

NEXT ROW: With RS facing, slip sts from first holder onto needle. Rejoin yarn and work on these 11 sts in garter stitch for 4 in. (10 cm), ending with a WS row. Break yarn, leaving tail to weave in.

Slip sts from second holder onto needle and knit across all 22 sts.

** Work even in garter stitch for 29$\frac{1}{2}$ in. (75 cm). BO.

1

2

3

4

MAKING THE SLIT

1 Work scarf up to * in pattern instructions (left), ending with wrong side row. Knit first 11 stitches on needle, then slip remaining 11 stitches onto stitch holder. Turn work and knit 4 in. (10 cm) of garter stitch on 11 stitches on needle, ending with wrong side row.

2 Slip stitches from needle onto second holder and break off yarn. Return stitches on first holder to needle. With right side facing, rejoin yarn and knit in garter stitch for 4 in. (10 cm), ending with wrong side row. Break off yarn.

3 With wrong side of both strips facing you, return stitches on second holder to needle. There are now 22 stitches on needle.

4 With right side of scarf facing, rejoin yarn at side edge and knit across all 22 stitches on needle. Work even in garter stitch, following pattern instructions from **.

octopus

scarf with tie ends

There are lots of ways to wear the Octopus scarf. Wind it around your neck and leave the tie ends hanging loose, braid them together, or knot them in a variety of combinations.

YOU WILL NEED

- 2 balls of pure wool chunky yarn with approx 100 yds (92 m) per 100 g ball
- Pair of size $10^1/_2$ (6.5 mm) knitting needles or size needed to achieve gauge
- 2 stitch holders
- Yarn needle

FINISHED SIZE

Scarf measures 4 in. (10 cm) wide and 55 in. (140 cm) long, including ties.

GAUGE

22 stitches and 18 rows to 4 in. (10 cm) measured over double rib, slightly stretched.

KNITTING THE SCARF

MAKE BEGINNING TIES

CO 8 sts.

ROW 1: (RS) K3, P2, K3.

** ROW 2: K1, P2, K2, P2, K1.

Rep Rows 1 and 2 28 times more, then rep Row 1 once more ***.

Make 3 ties, putting the first 2 ties onto stitch holders and leaving the last tie on the needle.

With WS of all the ties facing, slip the first 2 ties back onto the needle. (24 sts)

WORK BODY OF SCARF

FIRST ROW: **** (WS) K1, * P2, K2; rep from * to last 3 sts, P2, K1.

NEXT ROW: K3, * P2, K2; rep from * to last 5 sts, P 2, K3.

Rep these 2 rows until scarf measures approximately 42 in. (107 cm) from ends of ties, ending with a WS row.

DIVIDE FOR THE END TIES

NEXT ROW: (RS) K3, P2, K3.

Slip rem 16 sts onto holder.

Working on 8 sts on needle, complete first tie by working from ** to ***, then BO.

Transfer next 8 sts from holder to needle, rejoin yarn with RS facing and work to match first tie.

Transfer rem 8 sts from holder to needle and work to match first tie.

Prefer the bag? **see page 25 for the basic pattern**

1

2

3

MAKING THE TIES

1 Make 3 identical ties as given in pattern instructions (left), breaking off yarn after knitting each one. Slip first and second ties onto stitch holders, but leave third tie on knitting needle.

2 Turn needle so wrong side of third tie is facing you and transfer other 2 ties from stitch holders to same needle, making sure all ties face same way.

3 Once all 3 ties are on needle, rejoin yarn and work body of scarf from **** in pattern instructions, ending with wrong side row.

4 To make second set of ties, work across first 8 stitches on left needle in pattern and slip remaining 16 stitches onto holder. Complete first tie over 8 stitches as instructed.

5 Transfer next 8 stitches from holder to needle, rejoin yarn and work second tie to match first. Repeat with remaining 8 stitches to make third tie.

4

5

knotty bag

Use the basic Buttonhole Bag pattern, omitting the buttonhole, and make a tie on each piece like this: BO 30 sts along top edge to leave 12 sts on needle. Work in rib for 70 rows (RS rows: K3, P2, K2, P2, K3; WS rows: K1, * P2, K2; rep from * once, P2, K1) and BO. Stitch the bag pieces together and knot the ties to make a handle.

tab

scarf with tab-and-buckle fastening

This short scarf fastens with an ingenious knitted tab decorated with a buckle. To wear, tuck the plain end of the scarf behind the tab and adjust it to get a snug fit around your neck.

YOU WILL NEED

- 2 balls of pure wool chunky yarn with approx 100 yds (92 m) per 100 g ball
- Leftovers of the same yarn in a contrasting color
- Pair of size 8 (5 mm) and size 10½ (6.5 mm) knitting needles or size needed to achieve gauge
- Slot-through buckle about 1½ in. (4 cm) in diameter
- Yarn needle

FINISHED SIZE

Scarf measures 6 in. (15 cm) wide and 39 in. (100 cm) long.

GAUGE

14 stitches and 25 rows to 4 in. (10 cm) over garter stitch using size 10½ (6.5 mm) needles.

KNITTING THE SCARF

Knit and finish the scarf following the basic pattern on page 25, making it approximately 39 in. (100 cm) long. Make the tab fastening in contrast yarn as shown at right.

MAKING THE TAB FASTENING

1 With contrasting yarn and size 8 (5 mm) needles, cast on 7 stitches, leaving long yarn tail. Work in seed stitch (page 17) until tab is slightly longer than width of scarf. Bind off, leaving long yarn tail.

2 Slide buckle onto right side of tab and ease it into center of tab.

3 Mark position of tab on right side of scarf with 2 pins, positioning them about 6 in. (15 cm) from end of scarf.

4 Using yarn tails, stitch ends of tab to edges of scarf.

buckled bag

Two tabs with buckles make a stylish fastening for the plain Buttonhole Bag. Stitch the bound-off end of the tabs to the bound-off edge of the bag back. Secure the buckled end of the tabs with snaps stitched onto the back of the tabs and front of the bag.

kate

bag with grab handles

This sturdy, garter stitch bag can be knit in wool or cotton yarn and will stretch to hold a surprising amount. In the variation opposite, the basic pattern is transformed into a handy shoulder bag.

YOU WILL NEED

- 2 balls of pure wool chunky yarn with approx 100 yds (92 m) per 100 g ball
- Leftovers of the same yarn in a contrasting color
- Pair of size 9 (5.5 mm) and size 10 (6 mm) knitting needles or size needed to achieve gauge
- Sewing thread and sewing needle
- Yarn needle

FINISHED SIZE

Bag measures 9 in. (23 cm) deep, not including handles, and 10$\frac{1}{2}$ in. (27 cm) wide

GAUGE

15 stitches and 26 rows to 4 in. (10 cm) over garter stitch using size 10 (6 mm) needles

KNITTING THE BAG

CO 42 sts with size 10 (6 mm) needles following the basic pattern on page 25. Work the back and front in garter stitch for 66 rows, omitting the buttonhole and ending with a WS row. BO.

Tip
Seed stitch makes good, strong handles that keep their shape. Other suitable handle stitches are single rib (page 16) and moss stitch, used in the Shoulder Bag variation, right.

Prefer the shoulder bag? **see page 25 for the basic pattern**

MAKING THE HANDLES

1 With contrast yarn and size 9 (5.5 mm) needles, cast on 5 stitches, leaving long yarn tail. Work in seed stitch until strip measures 10 in. (25 cm) ending with right side row. Bind off, leaving long yarn tail. Make second handle to match first.

2 Mark position of handles on bag front. Insert 2 pins, each about 3 in. (8 cm) away from side edges. Pins mark outer edge of handle.

3 Pin ends of handle to bag front, making sure bound-off edge of front overlaps handle ends slightly, and outer edges of handle align with pins.

4 Using yarn tails, backstitch ends of handle to bag front by sewing through bag below bound-off stitches. Work 2 or 3 rows of stitches to make sure handle is firmly fixed. Repeat to match on bag back.

shoulder bag

Knit the basic Buttonhole Bag pattern in stockinette stitch, omitting the buttonhole row. Make a shoulder strap like this: CO 9 sts and work 45 in. (115 cm) in moss stitch (ROWS 1 and 3: * K1, P1; rep from * to last st, K1. ROWS 2 and 4: P1, * K1, P1; rep to end. Repeat Rows 1 to 4). BO. Overlap ends of strap with side seams of RS of bag for 1 in. (2.5 cm) and stitch securely in place.

susie

felted bag with drawstring handles

This felted bag is the perfect size for holding keys, cell phone, coin purse, cosmetics, and other essentials. The drawstring handles hold the top of the bag closed and are long enough to slip comfortably over a shoulder.

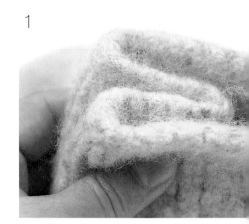

YOU WILL NEED

- 2 balls of pure wool chunky tweed yarn with approx 109 yds (100 m) per 100 g ball
- 1 ball of variegated handspun Aran weight yarn in a contrasting color with approx 109 yds (100 m) per 50 g ball
- Pair of size 10¹⁄₂ (7.5 mm) knitting needles or size needed to achieve gauge
- Large wooden knitting needle with sharp point
- Knitting nancy (or knitting spool)
- Yarn needle

FINISHED SIZE

Bag measures 9 in. (23 cm) deep and 12 in. (30 cm) wide after felting.

GAUGE

Working to an exact gauge is not necessary when making a felted bag. Knit a gauge swatch using the stated needles and machine wash it in hot water. The knit fabric should feel thick and substantial and have lost some stitch definition, but still be pliable. You may need to knit several swatches using different needle sizes to get a felted fabric that feels right. There's more information about felting on pages 112 and 113.

KNITTING THE BAG

Knit the bag following the basic pattern on page 25, omitting the buttonhole.

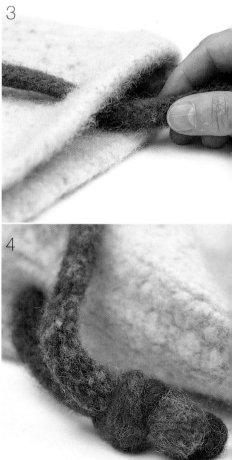

KNITTING THE HANDLES

Using the contrasting yarn, make a length of French knitting 78 in. (2 m) long following the instructions on page 45.

FINISHING THE BAG

Finish the bag as described in the basic pattern, omitting pressing. Machine wash the bag and handle in hot water and spin dry. Pull gently into shape and lay flat until completely dry.

Prefer the mittens? see page 26 for the basic pattern

ATTACHING THE HANDLES

1 Fold large inverted pleat at one side of top of bag.

2 Force wooden knitting needle through layers of pleat to make hole right through bag. Repeat Steps 1 and 2 at other side of bag.

3 Cut handle into two equal lengths. Slip first handle through holes in front of bag, leaving ends hanging in pleat at side. Slip other handle through holes in back of bag in same way.

4 Knot handle ends securely together at sides of bag. Pull handles to draw bag up so knots are hidden in pleats.

pompom mittens

Weave lengths of French knit cords between the stitches of a pair of basic Mittens, just above the cuffs. Decorate the ends of the cords with contrasting pompoms made following the instructions on page 31, and tie the cord ends in bows.

honey

bag with faux tortoiseshell handles

Ready-made bag handles are available in many different styles and finishes. Faux tortoiseshell handles work well with this bag, but the Honey bag would look equally attractive with bamboo or painted wooden handles.

YOU WILL NEED

- 4 balls of novelty felt finish chunky yarn with approx 55 yds (50 m) per 100 g ball
- Pair of size 10½ (6.5 mm) knitting needles or size needed to achieve gauge
- Pair of oval faux tortoiseshell bag handles
- Tapestry wool to match yarn
- Yarn needle

FINISHED SIZE

Bag measures 11 in. (28 cm) deep, not including handles, and 13½ in. (34 cm) wide.

GAUGE

12 stitches and 24 rows to 4 in. (10 cm) over garter stitch.

KNITTING THE BAG

CO 42 sts with size 10½ (6.5 mm) needles following the basic pattern on page 25.

Work the back and front in garter stitch for 56 rows, omitting the buttonhole and ending with a WS row.

SHAPE TOP

** BO 8 sts, knit to end of row. (34 sts) Turn, BO 8 sts purlwise, knit to end of row. (26 sts)

DECREASE ROW: (RS) * K2tog, K1; rep to last 2 sts, K2tog. (17 sts)

*** Working on these 17 sts, knit 9 more rows without shaping, ending with a WS row. BO.

FINISHING THE BAG

Finish the bag as described in the basic pattern on page 25.

APPLYING THE HANDLES

1 Work bag up to ** in pattern instructions (left), ending with wrong side row. Bind off 8 stitches at beginning of next row. Knit to end of row and turn.

2 Bind off 8 stitches at beginning of next row, but this time purl the stitches you are binding off instead of knitting them. Knit to end of row. There are now 26 stitches on needle.

3 Reduce number of stitches on needle to 17 by working knit 2 together, knit 1 alternately until last 2 stitches are reached. Knit these 2 stitches together, then follow pattern instructions from ***.

4 To attach handles, fold top of bag over handle and wrong side of knitting. Pin in place.

5 Using matching tapestry yarn, stitch bound-off edge of bag in place with small stitches. Fasten off yarn ends securely.

1

2

3

4

5

loopy

mittens with loop-and-button fastening

A series of stitched loops makes a lovely fastening for an accessory. Make the loops in matching yarn and choose pretty, ball-shaped buttons with a shank on the back to hold them above the loops.

YOU WILL NEED

- 2 [2, 3] balls of pure wool double knitting yarn with approx 131 yds (120 m) per 50 g ball
- Pair of size 8 (5 mm) and size 9 (5.5 mm) knitting needles or size needed to achieve gauge
- 6 decorative ball buttons with shank
- Yarn needle

NOTE

Yarn is used double throughout.

FINISHED SIZES

To fit women's sizes Small, Medium, Large (instructions for Medium and Large sizes are given in square brackets).

GAUGE

15 stitches and 20 rows to 4 in. (10 cm) over stockinette stitch using size 9 (5.5 mm) needles.

KNITTING THE MITTENS

Using two strands of yarn, knit the mittens following the basic pattern on page 26. Join the seams, omitting the cuff seam.

Prefer the scarf? see page 25 for the basic pattern

MAKING THE BUTTON LOOPS

1 Join a single length of yarn at cast-on edge on back of mitten and make stitch into edge about ¹/₂ in. (1 cm) away. Tighten yarn to leave loop around finger. Loop should be slightly larger than button so button can pass easily through it.

2 Work 2 or 3 more loops in same section of cuff, ending with yarn at left-hand edge of loops. Take small stitch through edge of knitting to secure loops.

3 Work series of blanket stitches (page 115) over yarn loops, working stitches close together so loops are completely covered with stitching.

4 Repeat along cuff to make 3 loops. Sew buttons onto opposite side of cuff to match loops.

buttoned scarf

Make a pair of button loops along one edge of a short garter stitch Scarf. Sew large decorative buttons with shanks on the opposite edge of the scarf, then fasten to make a cozy muffler.

zippy

shortie mittens with zipper

A matching zipper makes a neat, unobtrusive fastening for mittens. Knit an ordinary rib cuff and insert the zipper into the seam, or make a shortie version as shown.

YOU WILL NEED

- 1 [1, 2] balls of pure wool chunky yarn with approx 100 yds (92 m) per 100 g ball
- Pair of size 8 (5 mm) and size 9 (5.5 mm) knitting needles or size needed to achieve gauge
- Two 4 in. (10 cm) lightweight zippers to match yarn
- Matching embroidery floss
- Crewel embroidery needle
- Yarn needle

FINISHED SIZES

To fit women's sizes Small, Medium, Large (instructions for Medium and Large sizes are given in square brackets).

GAUGE

15 stitches and 20 rows to 4 in. (10 cm) over stockinette stitch using size 9 (5.5 mm) needles.

KNITTING THE MITTENS

Using size 8 (5 mm) needles, CO 34 [38, 42] sts.

ROWS 1 and 3: (RS) * K2, P2; rep from * to last 2 sts, K2.

ROWS 2 and 4: K1, P1, * K2, P2; rep from * to last 4 sts, K2, P1, K1.

Change to size 9 (5.5 mm) needles.

Beg with a knit (RS) row, work 2 [2, 4] rows in St st.

Follow the basic pattern on page 26, working from "Shape thumb gusset" to end.

Prefer the bag? **see page 25 for the basic pattern**

INSERTING THE ZIPPER

1 Join thumb seam of mitten, then join side seam, leaving 4 in. (10 cm) opening at base of seam to accommodate zipper.

2 Turn mitten to right side. With zipper closed and the pull at cuff edge, pin one side of zipper to edge of opening, folding end of tape beyond pull to wrong side. Repeat, pinning other side of zipper to opposite side of opening.

3 Using 2 strands of matching embroidery floss in crewel needle, backstitch zipper in place along both sides of opening.

zipper bag

Add a zippered pocket to the front of the Buttonhole Bag. Omit the buttonhole and add tie handles from page 57. Knit a seed stitch (page 17) pocket in two pieces, making a shallow piece for the top and a deeper piece for the base. Stitch the bound-off edges together at the sides, leaving a long opening between the pieces, and insert a matching zipper in the opening. Stitch all four edges to the bag.

anna

hat with earflaps and cords

This hat is great fun to wear. Leave the earflaps and cords loose, tie the cords together under your chin to keep your ears warm, or knot them on top of your head to make a traditional deerstalker hat!

YOU WILL NEED:

- 2 balls of pure wool chunky yarn with approx 100 yds (92 m) per 100 g
- Pair of size 8 (5 mm), size 10 (6 mm) and size 10¹/₂ (7 mm) knitting needles or size needed to achieve gauge
- Crochet hook
- Yarn needle

FINISHED SIZE

Hat measures 8 in. (20 cm) deep and 18 in. (46 cm) in circumference. Earflaps and cords measure 15 in. (38 cm) long, not including tassels.

GAUGE

16 stitches and 22 rows to 4 in. (10 cm) over stockinette stitch using size 10 (6 mm) needles.

KNITTING THE HAT

Knit and finish the hat following the basic pattern on page 27, changing to stockinette stitch to work the rest of the hat after the first 4 rows of double rib have been worked.

EARFLAPS (make two)

CO 14 sts using size 8 (5 mm) needles. Work 14 rows in garter stitch.

** DECREASE ROW: (RS) Knit to last 3 sts, K2tog, K1.

Rep decrease row until 3 sts rem, ending with a RS row.

CORD ROW 1: (WS) K1, P1, K1.

CORD ROW 2: K3.

Rep these 2 rows until cord is approximately 12 in. (30 cm) long, ending with a WS row.

NEXT ROW: K2tog, K1. (2 sts)

NEXT ROW: K2tog.

Fasten off yarn.

Tip

Want to be more colorful? Use contrasting yarns in different colors to knit each earflap, then change the yarn color again to knit the cords. You can also add contrasting yarn to the tassels.

Prefer the bag? **see page 25 for the basic pattern**

1

2

3

4

5

MAKING THE EARFLAPS

1 Work earflap up to ** in pattern instructions (left), ending with wrong side row. Shape earflap by knitting to last 3 stitches, knitting next 2 stitches together and knitting last stitch. Do this on every row until 3 stitches remain on needle.

2 Make cord by repeating both cord pattern rows until cord measures 12 in. (30 cm) long.

3 To shape end of cord, knit first 2 stitches together and knit last stitch. On next row, knit remaining 2 stitches together and fasten off yarn by pulling it through remaining stitch.

4 Cut 3 or 4 lengths of yarn and loop them through end of cord with crochet hook. Adjust lengths so yarn ends are even.

5 Tie yarn in overhand knot, making sure knot rests against end of cord. Trim yarn ends neatly.

ATTACHING THE EARFLAPS

Pin earlaps to each side of the hat. Try on the hat in front of a mirror and adjust the position of the earflaps if necessary. Using an overcast seam, stitch the earflaps to the cast-on edge of the hat.

buttoned bag

Make a flap fastening for the Buttonhole Bag by working an earflap with a 2¹⁄₂ in. (6.5 cm) cord, leaving a long yarn tail. Fold the cord in half to make a loop and wrap the tail around the cord four or five times to secure the loop. Fasten off the yarn end on the back of the flap. Stitch the flap to the back of the bag, centering it on the buttonhole. Stitch a button on the front of the bag to correspond with the loop.

heidi

rib hat with braided ties

Lengths of yarn from the same color palette are combined to make simple braided ties. You can make the ties wider by adding more lengths of yarn to the hat before you start plaiting.

YOU WILL NEED:

- 1 ball of pure wool chunky yarn with approx 100 yds (92 m) per 100 g
- Leftovers of coordinating double knitting or worsted weight yarns
- Pair of size 10 (6 mm) and size 10¹/₂ (7 mm) knitting needles or size needed to achieve gauge
- Yarn needle

FINISHED SIZE

Hat measures 8 in. (20 cm) deep and 18 in. (46 cm) in circumference. The braids measure 11 in. (28 cm) long.

GAUGE

16 stitches and 18 rows to 4 in. (10 cm) measured over double rib, slightly stretched widthways, using size 10 (6 mm) needles.

KNITTING THE HAT

Knit and finish the hat following the basic pattern on page 27.

MAKING THE BRAIDS

1 Mark position of braid at each side of hat with loop of yarn. Cut nine 39 in. (1 m) lengths of different yarns for each braid. Thread braid lengths through hat at marked point, using yarn needle to thread 3 lengths through at a time.

2 When all strands have been threaded through, adjust so ends are even. Divide braid strands with your fingers into 3 groups of 6 strands.

3 Plait strands together, working at alternate sides and moving each outside group of strands into center of braid. Continue until braid is about 10 in. (25 cm) long.

4 Tie end of braid in overhand knot, making sure knot rests against end of braid. Trim ends neatly to make tassel.

Tip

Combining mohair, ribbon, metallic, and highly textured yarns with several strands of the hat yarn will make fat, chunky braids.

Prefer the scarf? **see page 25 for the basic pattern**

braided scarf

Add braids to corners of the basic garter stitch Scarf, mixing light and dark shades of scarf color. Wear the scarf with braids hanging loose or knot them together in pairs or in a group of four.

bluebell

capelet with ribbon ties

This plain capelet is trimmed with narrow ribs along the top and bottom edges and will sit snugly around your shoulders. It fastens with a generous bow of matching double satin ribbon.

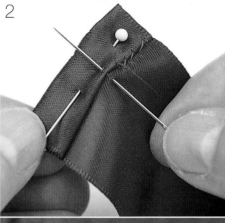

YOU WILL NEED

- 3 balls of pure wool chunky yarn with 87 yds (80 m) per 100 g
- Pair of size 10¹/₂ (6.5 mm) knitting needles or size needed to achieve gauge
- 60 in. (152 cm) of 1¹/₂ in. (4 cm) wide matching satin ribbon
- Matching sewing thread and sewing needle
- Yarn needle

FINISHED SIZE

Capelet measures 8 in. (20 cm) deep and 48 in. (122 cm) in circumference along lower edge from front to back. The ties measure 28 in. (71 cm) long.

GAUGE

13 stitches and 18 rows to 4 in. (10 cm) measured over stockinette stitch.

KNITTING THE PANELS
(make two)

CO 75 sts following the basic pattern on page 27.

ROWS 1, 3, and 5: * K1, P1; rep to last st, K1.

ROWS 2 and 4: * P1, K1; rep from * to last st, P1.

SHAPE BACK AND FRONT EDGES

Work Rows 6 to 19 as given in the basic pattern on page 27.

SHAPE SHOULDER

Work Rows 1 to 9 as given in the basic pattern.

ROW 10: * K1, P1; rep to last st, K1.

ROW 11: * P1, K1; rep to last st, P1.

ROW 12: * K1, P1; rep to last st, K1. BO.

FINISHING THE CAPELET

Finish the capelet as described in the basic pattern, omitting the ties.

ATTACHING THE RIBBON TIES

1 Cut ribbon into 2 equal pieces. Fold over ¹/₂ in. (1 cm) of raw edge onto right side at 1 short end of ribbon, then fold over again to make double hem that folds onto right side of ribbon.

2 Pin hem in place then secure by stitching across folded edge using matching sewing thread.

3 Pin right side of hemmed end of tie to wrong side of each front edge at neckline overlapping them so hem on ribbon is hidden. Use matching thread to stitch securely to capelet.

4 Using sharp scissors, cut other end of ties on diagonal to make neat points.

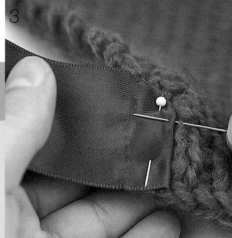

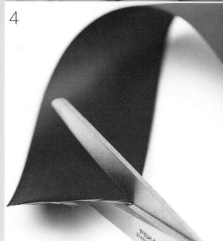

chapter 4
beading and embellishing

Our five **funky accessories** lend themselves well to the addition of a little glitz and glamour. From silver and gold **pebble** beads to delicate **pearl** buttons, the potential for adding decorative details to the basic patterns is endless. In this section, beads are both attached to the surface of finished accessories and knitted in. **Glass cube** beads look fabulous arranged in **spiral shapes** on a felted buttonhole bag, while **chunky beads** make a fun finish for a fringed scarf. In Pearl, mother-of-pearl buttons transform a plain bag into a purse to die for. But this chapter is not just about buttons and beads: turn to page 88 for our **slashed felted bag** and scarf.

swirl

scarf with beaded spirals

Spiral shapes made from tiny beads are randomly scattered across the ends of this plain scarf. Combine several colors of beads in each spiral or work them in a single color.

YOU WILL NEED

- 2 balls of pure wool chunky yarn with approx 100 yds (92 m) per 100 g ball
- Pair of size 10½ (6.5 mm) knitting needles or size needed to achieve gauge
- Embroidery floss to match yarn
- Small glass seed beads in green, orange, blue, and red (approx 48 of each color)
- Crewel embroidery needle
- Yarn needle

FINISHED SIZE

Scarf measures 6 in. (15 cm) wide and 70 in. (178 cm) long.

GAUGE

14 stitches and 18 rows to 4 in. (10 cm) measured over stockinette stitch.

KNITTING THE SCARF

CO 22 sts following the basic pattern on page 25.

ROW 1: (RS) Knit.

ROW 2: K1, P to last st, K1.

Rep Rows 1 and 2 until the scarf is approximately 70 in. (178 cm) long, ending with a WS row. BO.

Weave in the yarn ends and press lightly on the wrong side.

Cut several 39 in. (1 m) lengths of matching embroidery floss and divide each piece of floss into single strands of thread. Fold one strand in half and insert the cut ends through the crewel needle. Use the loop method shown on page 87 to secure the thread on the wrong side of the scarf.

Prefer the bag? **see page 25 for the basic pattern**

BEADING THE SPIRALS

1 Begin at center of spiral. Bring needle through scarf, slip green bead onto thread so it rests on knitting. Take stitch through knitting, bringing needle through short distance in front of bead. Make sure needle comes through knitted stitch, not through hole between stitches.

2 Slip orange bead onto thread so it rests on knitting. Take stitch through knitting back toward previous bead, bringing the needle through in front of orange bead.

3 Working in curved line, attach a blue bead then a red bead to complete color sequence.

4 Continue to attach beads in curved line, working outward from center of spiral and following same color sequence. To finish spiral, take thread through to wrong side and secure by working a few stitches into back of knitting. Work 3 or 4 spirals at each end of scarf.

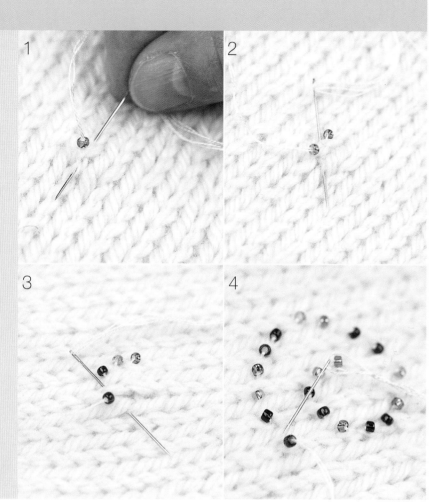

spiral bag

Felted knitting and shiny beads have attractively contrasting textures. Combine felted Icelandic wool with spirals of iridescent glass cube beads to make this pretty and unusual bag.

firefly

scarf with knitted-in beads

Chunky beads with a metallic finish sparkle against a dark background color. The beads are knitted in as you go, so make sure you thread them onto the yarn before starting to knit.

YOU WILL NEED

- 2 balls of pure wool chunky yarn with approx 100 yds (92 m) per 100 g ball
- Pair of size 10 (6 mm) knitting needles or size needed to achieve gauge
- 40 chunky metallic beads with hole large enough to accommodate yarn
- Yarn needle

FINISHED SIZE

Scarf measures 6 in. (15 cm) wide and 48 in. (122 cm) long.

GAUGE

15 stitches and 24 rows to 4 in. (10 cm) measured over pattern.

SPECIAL ABBREVIATION FOR THIS PATTERN

B = apply bead.

PREPARING THE YARN

Before starting to knit, thread 20 beads onto each ball of yarn.

KNITTING THE SCARF

CO 22 sts following the basic pattern on page 25, but using size 10 (6 mm) needles.

WORK BEADED BORDER

** ROW 1: (RS, ridge row) K1, P to last st, K1.

ROWS 2, 4, and 6: Rep Row 1.

ROW 3: Knit.

ROW 5: (bead row) K3, B, *K4, B; rep from * to last 3 sts, K3.

ROW 6: K1, P to last st, K1.

Rep Rows 1 to 6 four times more, ending with a Row 6 ***.

WORK SECTION WITHOUT BEADS

ROW 1: (RS, ridge row) K1, P to last st, K1.

ROWS 2, 4, and 6: Rep Row 1.

ROWS 3 and 5: Knit.

ROW 6: K1, P to last st, K1.

Rep Rows 1 to 6 thirty times more, ending with a Row 6.

WORK BEADED BORDER

Rep from ** to ***.

NEXT ROW: (ridge row) K1, P to last st, K1. BO.

WORKING THE BEADING

1 Thread 20 beads individually onto each ball of yarn using yarn needle that fits through beads. Push beads down yarn for several yards to leave enough yarn to cast on and work first few rows of pattern.

2 If beads have holes that are too small to accommodate yarn thickness, thread them onto loop of finer yarn. Loop bead and knitting yarn together as shown, then slide beads from bead yarn onto knitting yarn and move them along yarn as above.

3 Following pattern instructions, knit to position of first bead. Bring yarn between needles to front of work and slip first bead on yarn so it rests snugly against knitting.

4 Slip next stitch purlwise and, holding bead at front of work, move yarn to back of work and knit to position of next bead. Repeat Steps 3 and 4 along row.

5 On next row, purl slipped stitches as usual, taking care that beads do not slip through to wrong side of knitting.

FINISHING THE SCARF

Weave in the yarn ends on the wrong side. Block if necessary using the cold water method described on page 23.

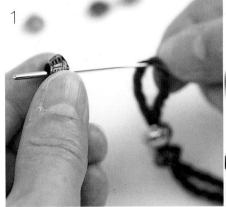

1

2

3

4

5

charming

scarf with charms and bells

Glass and plastic heart charms are randomly scattered across the ends of a plain scarf to make a deep border. Combine the hearts with tiny gold- and silver-colored bells to finish the decoration.

YOU WILL NEED

- 2 balls of pure wool chunky yarn with approx 100 yds (92 m) per 100 g ball
- Pair of size 10½ (6.5 mm) knitting needles or size needed to achieve gauge
- Embroidery floss to match yarn
- Selection of glass and plastic heart charms and tiny metal bells
- Crewel embroidery needle
- Yarn needle

FINISHED SIZE

Scarf measures 6 in. (15 cm) wide and 70 in. (178 cm) long.

GAUGE

14 stitches and 18 rows to 4 in. (10 cm) measured over stockinette stitch.

KNITTING THE SCARF

CO 22 sts following the basic pattern on page 25.

ROW 1: (RS) Knit.

ROW 2: K1, P to last st, K1.

Rep Rows 1 and 2 until the scarf is approximately 70 in. (178 cm) long, ending with a WS row. BO.

Weave in the yarn ends and press lightly on the wrong side.

Cut several 20 in. (50 cm) lengths of matching embroidery floss and divide each piece of floss into single strands of thread. Fold the strand in half and insert the cut ends through the crewel needle. Use the loop method shown on page 87 to secure the thread on the wrong side of the scarf.

APPLYING THE CHARMS AND BELLS

1 Attach heart charms with vertical hole through center by working 2 or 3 long vertical stitches through hole and through scarf. Secure thread on wrong side after attaching each heart.

2 Attach heart charms with 2 or more holes through edge by working 2 or 3 stitches through holes and through scarf. Secure each piece of thread on wrong side.

3 Attach heart charms with loop by working 2 or 3 stitches through hole and into scarf. Secure each piece of thread on wrong side.

4 Scatter hearts at random in band across each end of scarf. To finish, sew some small bells between hearts securing each bell with several stitches through loop and into scarf.

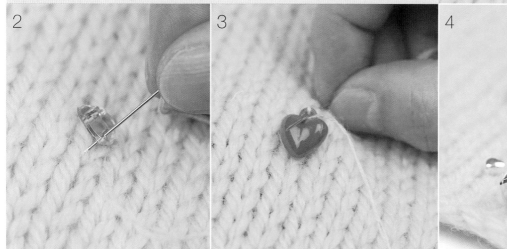

shamrock hat

Originally made to embellish cross stitch embroidery, metal charms come in a variety of shapes and finishes. Shamrock charms make the perfect decoration for the cuff of the Jaunty hat from page 46.

Tip

Beading and embroidery stores have dazzling arrays of embellishments with which to adorn your knitting. Choose lightweight charms so your knitting doesn't pull out of shape.

flora

bag with knitted ball buttons

Turn large round beads into funky buttons by covering each one with a strip of knitting. Arrange the buttons to make a flower shape to liven up the front of a plain shoulder bag.

buttoned mittens

Cover beads with strips knit from variegated yarn and use them to decorate plain Mittens. Group three buttons above the rib cuff or arrange several in a line down the back of the mitten in the same way as the shank buttons on page 92.

Prefer the mittens? see page 26 for the basic pattern

YOU WILL NEED

- 2 balls of pure wool chunky yarn with approx 100 yds (92 m) per 100 g ball
- Pair of size 5 (3.75 mm) and size 10 (6 mm) knitting needles or size needed to achieve gauge
- Leftovers of contrasting double knitting yarn in 2 colors
- 7 lightweight wooden or plastic beads, approximately $^3/_4$ in. (2 mm) in diameter
- Yarn needle

FINISHED SIZE

Bag measures $9^1/_2$ in. (24 cm) deep and $11^1/_2$ in. (29 cm) wide, not including strap.

GAUGE

15 stitches and 19 rows to 4 in. (10 cm) measured over stockinette stitch using size 10 (6 mm) needles.

KNITTING THE BAG

Using size 10 (6 mm) needles, knit the back and front of the bag following the basic pattern on page 25, omitting the buttonhole. Make the strap by following the instructions for the Shoulder Bag variation on page 61.

1

3

2

4

MAKING KNITTED BUTTONS

1 Cast on 6 stitches on size 5 (3.75 mm) needles using contrast double knitting weight yarn. Work about 10 rows of stockinette stitch or until strip fits snugly around bead. Bind off. Make 6 strips in first color and 1 strip in second color.

2 To make each button, wrap knitted strip around bead. Using one of yarn tails, sew the cast-on edge of the strip to the bound-off edge.

3 Holding bead in position, use same yarn tail to stitch from side to side of strip so it covers one side of bead. Secure yarn tail by slipping it through knitting and bringing it out in center of seam.

4 Turn bead over and use remaining yarn tail to stitch strip over other end of bead. Secure this yarn tail in same way as above. Using photograph as guide to position, use yarn tails to stitch buttons to front of bag.

pearl

bag with mother-of-pearl buttons

Pearl buttons make a fantastic embellishment for a plain stockinette stitch bag worked in a dark yarn color. If you're buying the buttons, choose a variety of shapes and sizes for maximum impact or mix new and vintage buttons.

YOU WILL NEED

- 2 balls of pure wool chunky yarn with approx 100 yds (92 m) per 100 g ball
- Pair of size 10 (6 mm) knitting needles or size needed to achieve gauge
- Selection of pearl buttons in different shapes and sizes
- Embroidery floss in bright colors
- Crewel embroidery needle
- Yarn needle

FINISHED SIZE

Bag measures 9¹/₂ in. (24 cm) deep and 11¹/₂ in. (29 cm) wide.

GAUGE

15 stitches and 19 rows to 4 in. (10 cm) measured over stockinette stitch.

KNITTING THE BAG

Knit the back and front of the bag following the basic pattern on page 25.

DECORATING THE BAG

1 Cut several 20 in. (50 cm) lengths of brightly colored embroidery floss. Using your fingers, carefully divide each piece of floss into 3 sections, each containing 2 strands of floss.

2 Use 1 section of floss at a time. Fold floss in half and insert cut ends through crewel needle. On right side of bag front, take needle under knit stitch and pull floss through to leave short loop on surface.

3 Take needle through loop and pull floss gently to lock floss in place. Thread button onto needle and slide it along floss to rest flat on knitting.

4 Take stitch over center of button, going back through second hole in button and through knitting. Bring needle through first hole and make several more stitches until button is secure, then take needle through to wrong side and work 2 or 3 stitches through knitting at back of button to secure end.

5 Repeat Steps 2 to 4 to secure each button, mixing sizes and shapes of buttons and varying thread colors. Scatter buttons at random across bag front, keeping them below buttonhole.

jenny

felted bag with slashed pocket

Contrasting handles and a decoratively slashed pocket add unique touches to this felted bag. The matching scarf is both unusual and practical: it will keep you warm and is guaranteed not to fray.

YOU WILL NEED

- 2 balls of pure wool chunky tweed yarn with approx 109 yds (100 m) per 100 g ball
- Pair of size 10 (6 mm) and size 10¹/₂ (7.5 mm) knitting needles or size needed to achieve gauge
- Leftovers of variegated handspun Aran weight yarn in a similar colorway to the main yarn
- Leftovers of pure wool chunky yarn in solid color to match 1 of the colors in the variegated yarn
- Embroidery floss to match main yarn
- Crewel embroidery needle
- Yarn needle

FINISHED SIZE

Bag measures 9¹/₂ in. (24 cm) deep, not including handles, and 11¹/₂ in. (29 cm) wide.

GAUGE

Working to an exact gauge is not necessary when making a felted bag. Knit a gauge swatch using the stated needles and machine wash it in hot water. The knit fabric should feel thick and substantial and have lost some stitch definition, but still be pliable. You may need to knit several swatches using different needle sizes to get a felted fabric that feels right. There's more information about felting on pages 112 and 113.

KNITTING THE BAG

Using the size 10¹/₂ (7.5 mm) needles, knit and finish the bag following the basic pattern on page 25, omitting the buttonhole.

KNITTING THE POCKET

Using size 10 (6 mm) needles and the solid color yarn, CO 28 sts.
ROW 1: (RS) Knit.
ROW 2: K1, P to last st, K1.
Rep Rows 1 and 2 fourteen more times, ending with a WS row.
Break yarn, join in contrasting variegated yarn, and rep Rows 1 and 2 twice more. BO.

KNITTING THE HANDLES (make two)

Using size 10 (6 mm) needles and the contrasting variegated yarn, CO 6 sts. Work 120 rows of garter stitch. BO.

FINISHING THE BAG

Finish the bag as described in the basic pattern, omitting pressing. Machine wash the bag and handles in hot water and spin dry. Pull gently into shape and lay flat until completely dry. Repeat with the pocket, but this time use a warm wash.

slashed scarf

Knit the basic Scarf in stockinette stitch and machine wash it in hot water. Pull it into shape and allow to dry. Cut a series of 1 in. (2.5 cm) slashes all around the edge of the scarf, then machine wash again at the same temperature to open up the slashes.

Prefer the scarf? **see page 25 for the basic pattern**

FINISHING THE POCKET

1 After pocket has dried, cut series of 1 in. (2.5 cm) slashes into knitting along lower edge and both side edges. Felt pocket for second time by machine washing it in hot water. Ease it into shape and allow to dry.

2 Pin handles to top of bag, positioning 2 in. (5 cm) ends of handles on right side of bag. Stitch securely to bag using embroidery floss.

3 Pin pocket to front of bag, positioning pins along top edge and inside slashes on other 3 sides.

4 Using same embroidery floss, work row of large backstitches around 3 sides of pocket, positioning row of stitching a short distance inside slashes.

astra

mittens with starburst sequins

Sequins add instant glitz to the simplest of knitted accessories. Stitch them onto knitting with embroidery floss, arranging the sequins to make a pretty starburst pattern.

YOU WILL NEED

- 2 [2, 2] balls of pure wool chunky yarn with approx 100 yds (92 m) per 100 g ball
- Pair of size 8 (5 mm) and size 9 (5.5 mm) knitting needles or size needed to achieve gauge
- Selection of cup-shaped sequins in a variety of colors, approx $^3/_8$ in. (1 cm) in diameter
- Embroidery floss to match 1 of the sequin colors
- Crewel embroidery needle
- Yarn needle

FINISHED SIZES

To fit women's sizes Small, Medium, Large (instructions for Medium and Large sizes are given in square brackets).

GAUGE

15 stitches and 20 rows to 4 in. (10 cm) measured over stockinette stitch using size 9 (5.5 mm) needles.

KNITTING THE MITTENS

Using size 8 (5 mm) needles, CO 34 [38, 42] sts.

ROWS 1, 3, and 5: (RS) Knit.

ROWS 2 and 4: K1, P to last st, K1.

ROWS 6, 7, and 8: Knit.

Change to size 9 (5.5 mm) needles and stockinette stitch.

Beg with a knit (RS) row, work 4 [4, 6] rows of St st.

Follow the basic pattern on page 26, working from "Shape thumb gusset" to end.

APPLYING THE SEQUINS

1 Cut 20 in. (50 cm) length of embroidery floss and divide it into 2-strand sections. Thread cut ends of 1 section through crewel needle. On right side of back of 1 mitten, take needle under knit stitch and lock floss in place using loop method shown on page 87.

2 Slip sequin onto floss with concave side facing upward. Push sequin along floss so it rests on knitting.

3 Take stitch over sequin, going through knitting at edge of sequin and bringing needle through short distance away at edge of sequin.

4 Work several straight stitches over sequin, working from outside and going down through hole each time, so stitches radiate from center. Take needle through to wrong side and secure floss by working several stitches into knitting behind sequin. Repeat Steps 2 to 4 to secure each sequin, scattering them randomly across back of each mitten.

FINISHING THE MITTENS

Finish the mittens as described in the basic pattern, omitting the pressing as this may damage the sequins.

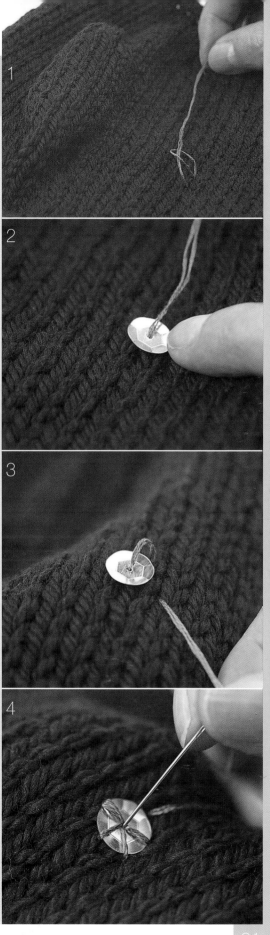

froggy

mittens with novelty buttons

A row of cartoon buttons looks bright and cheerful arranged in a line down the back of plain stockinette stitch mittens. Choose buttons with shanks, rather than the sew-through type, as these will stand up nicely off the knitted fabric.

YOU WILL NEED

- 2 [2, 2] balls of pure wool chunky yarn with approx 100 yds (92 m) per ,100 g ball
- Pair of size 8 (5 mm) and size 9 (5.5 mm) knitting needles or size needed to achieve gauge
- Leftovers of contrasting yarn
- 10 novelty buttons with shanks
- Embroidery floss to match main yarn color
- Crewel embroidery needle
- Yarn needle

FINISHED SIZES

To fit women's sizes Small, Medium, Large (instructions for Medium and Large sizes are given in square brackets).

GAUGE

15 stitches and 20 rows to 4 in. (10 cm) measured over stockinette stitch using size 9 (5.5 mm) needles.

KNITTING THE MITTENS

Knit the mittens following the basic pattern on page 26.

APPLYING THE BUTTONS

1 Thread length of contrasting yarn into yarn needle. Count stitches across back of mitten and use yarn to mark center of back by working line of large running stitches through center stitches. Mark position of buttons with pins, spacing them evenly in a row down knitting, following line of contrast stitching.

2 Cut 20 in. (50 cm) length of embroidery floss, divide into 2-strand sections and use loop method (page 87) to attach 1

section to one of positions marked by a pin. Remove pin, carefully snip contrast yarn and ease ends out of knitting using yarn needle.

3 Thread button onto needle, sliding it along floss to rest against knitting. Take several stitches over button shank and through knitting to fix in place.

4 Bring needle back through fabric close to shank, then wind floss 2 or 3 times around stitches beneath shank. Take

needle back through to wrong side and secure floss by working several stitches into knitting behind button. Repeat Steps 2 to 4 to secure remaining buttons.

FINISHING THE MITTENS
Finish the mittens as described in the basic pattern, omitting the pressing as this may damage the buttons.

fishy hat

Tiny shank buttons look great dotted over the basic Hat knit in double rib. Match the embroidery floss color to that of the yarn and use a separate length to stitch each button in place.

gretchen

hat with beaded ties

It's quick and easy to add simple beaded ties to hats and other accessories. Use chunky plastic craft beads to decorate the ties. They are lightweight, unbreakable, and come in a wide range of colors.

YOU WILL NEED

- 2 balls of pure wool chunky yarn with approx 100 yds (92 m) per 100 g ball
- Pair of size 10 (6 mm) and size 10¹/₂ (7 mm) knitting needles or size needed to achieve gauge
- Leftovers of contrasting yarn
- Pony beads with added glitter, approx ¹/₄ in. (8 mm) in diameter
- Yarn needle

FINISHED SIZE

Hat measures 8 in. (20 cm) deep and 18 in. (46 cm) in circumference. Beaded ties measure 11 in. (28 cm) long, not including tassels.

GAUGE

16 stitches and 22 rows to 4 in. (10 cm) over stockinette stitch using size 10 (6 mm) needles.

KNITTING THE HAT

Knit and finish the hat following the basic pattern on page 27. Change to stockinette stitch after working the first four rows of double rib.

BEADING THE TIES

1 Mark position of ties on hat with contrast yarn. Cut two 70 in. (180 cm) lengths of hat yarn to make ties. Thread 1 length into yarn needle and thread end of yarn through hat at marked point.

2 Unthread needle and pull yarn through knitting until ends are even. Remove yarn marker and tie overhand knot in yarn close to hat edge.

3 Thread pony bead onto 1 strand of yarn and tie overhand knot in both strands below bead to secure it. Repeat until beaded tie is desired length.

4 Trim ends of yarn evenly about 1 in. (2.5 cm) below final bead. Repeat for second tie.

fringed bag

Short beaded ties make an irregular fringe across the top of a Buttonhole Bag. Vary the lengths of the ties and attach them to the bag at random intervals, making sure you attach the center ties below the buttonhole.

twinkle

hat with beaded brim

Add sparkle to a ribbed hat by making a narrow brim and stitching a row of pretty beads around the edge. Choose clear, silver-lined beads that go with any yarn color or pick a contrasting color.

YOU WILL NEED

- 2 balls of pure wool chunky yarn with approx 100 yds (92 m) per 100 g ball
- Pair of size 10 (6 mm) and size 10½ (6.5 mm) knitting needles or size needed to achieve gauge
- Silver-lined glass pebble beads
- Tapestry wool to match yarn color
- Tapestry needle
- Yarn needle

FINISHED SIZE

Hat measures 9 in. (23 cm) deep and 18 in. (46 cm) in circumference.

GAUGE

16 stitches and 18 rows to 4 in. (10 cm) measured over double rib, slightly stretched widthwise, using size 10 (6 mm) needles.

KNITTING THE HAT

Using size 10½ (6.5 mm) needles, CO 72 sts.

Change to size 10 (6 mm) needles.

ROW 1: (RS of hat, WS of brim) Knit.

ROW 2: K1, P to last st, K1.

Rep Rows 1 and 2 once more.

Follow the basic pattern on page 27, working from Row 1 to the end.

BEADING THE BRIM

1 Cut 18 in. (45 cm) length of tapestry or double knitting yarn and thread into tapestry needle. Secure end of yarn by weaving it along edge on wrong side of hat.

2 Bring yarn out just below first row of purl stitches on hat brim. Thread bead onto needle and slide it along yarn to rest against knitting.

3 Take needle back through knitting above same purl stitch to make vertical stitch through bead and into knitting. Repeat along brim, applying 1 bead to every purl stitch.

4 When all beads have been applied, roll brim upward on right side of hat so cast-on edge is aligned with first row of rib stitches. Pin in place, positioning pins vertically.

5 Using same thread as used to apply beads, stitch edge of brim neatly to hat, taking care to work stitches fairly loosely so edge of hat remains stretchy. Join hat seam.

1

2

3

MAKING THE BEADED FRINGE

1 Cut eighty 12 in. (30 cm) lengths of tapestry wool to make fringe. Thread 1 length into tapestry needle and insert 1 end of yarn into bottom edge of capelet .

2 Unthread needle and pull yarn through knitting until ends are even. Tie overhand knot in yarn close to capelet edge. Repeat, spacing yarn fringes evenly along edge.

3 Thread selection of 3 or 4 beads onto each yarn fringe. Thread each piece of yarn into needle and take both strands separately through beads.

4 When beads have been threaded onto both strands of yarn, tie overhand knot in yarn below beads to secure them. Repeat along lower edge of capelet. Leave yarn strands untrimmed below beads.

4

beaded scarf

Knit the basic Scarf pattern in double rib and decorate each end with a randomly beaded fringe. Knot the yarn strands in pairs as if you were making a lattice fringe (page 33), add a bead, then knot each pair of strands again below the bead. Add a smaller bead to each single strand, and knot the yarn below each one, varying the lengths of the strands to give a random effect. Trim any surplus yarn below the beads.

chapter 5
customizing knitting

So far we have shown you how you can personalize a range of accessories by **changing the edgings** of accessories and **embellishing** them with handmade or store-bought trimmings and handles. In this chapter, you'll discover how **substituting yarns** and **stitches** can transform our five basic patterns. Try using **handspun** and **novelty** yarns, **felting** the accessories, or decorating them with simple **embroidery** stitches to stamp your own style on the pieces. By using some of the fun ideas from the earlier chapters too, you can make **one-of-a-kind pieces** that are truly your own creations.

foxy

long fingerless mittens

To make these fingerless mittens, follow the basic pattern on page 26. Stop knitting before you complete both thumb and main body of the mitten and work a few rib rows before binding off. If you wish, extend the mitten cuff to fit snugly up your forearm.

YOU WILL NEED

- 2 [2, 2] skeins of variegated handspun chunky yarn in 75% wool, 25% silk with approx 130 yds (120 m) per 100 g skein
- Pair of size 8 (5 mm) and size 9 (5.5 mm) knitting needles or size needed to achieve gauge
- Yarn needle

NOTE

When knitting with handspun yarn, you should be aware that the color sequence in each skein will be slightly different so your pair of mittens will not be an-exact match.

FINISHED SIZES

To fit women's sizes Small, Medium, Large (instructions for Medium and Large sizes are given in square brackets).

GAUGE

14 stitches and 23 rows to 4 in. (10 cm) over stockinette stitch using size 9 (5.5 mm) needles.

KNITTING THE MITTENS

Using size 9 (5.5 mm) needles, CO 43 [49, 55] sts.

ROW 1: (RS) K1, * P1, K1; rep from * to end.

ROW 2: * P1, K1; rep from * to last st, P1.

Rep Rows 1 and 2 once more.

Cont working in single rib, dec 1 st at each end of next and every foll 4th row until there are 29 [33, 37] sts on needle.

Work 4 more rows of single rib, ending with a RS row.

NEXT ROW: Rib 6 sts, M1, (rib 4 [5, 6] sts, M1) 4 times, rib 7 sts. (34 [38, 42] sts)

Change to stockinette stitch (RS rows knit, WS rows purl).

Beg with a knit row, work 4 [4, 6] rows of St st.

Follow the basic pattern from ** to ***.

NEXT ROW: P11 [13, 13], turn.

Working on these 11 [13, 13] sts only, work 0 [2, 4] rows without shaping.

Change to size 8 (5 mm) needles and work 4 rows of single rib.

BO in rib.

With RS facing, rejoin yarn at base of thumb. Change to size 9 (5.5 mm) needles and knit to end of row. (33 [35, 39] sts)

Work 5 [7, 9] rows of stockinette stitch without shaping.

Change to size 8 (5 mm) needles and work 4 [5, 6] rows of single rib.

BO in rib.

WORKING
THE MITTENS

1 Cast on number of stitches for your size. To work arm shaping at beginning of each decrease row, knit first stitch, then knit next 2 stitches together to decrease 1 stitch.

2 Work across row in single rib until you reach last 3 stitches. Slip first stitch as if going to knit, knit next stitch then pass slipped stitch over knitted stitch to decrease 1 stitch. Knit last stitch.

3 Follow pattern instructions until you reach ***, then transfer stitches on right needle onto waste yarn. Purl correct number of stitches for your size, then slip stitches on left needle onto another piece of waste yarn. Follow pattern instructions to complete thumb, changing to size 8 (5 mm) needles to work rib rows.

4 To bind off thumb stitches in rib, knit each knit stitch and purl each purl stitch along row, binding them off in usual way.

bella

recyled fabric bag

Fabric strips joined together make a good yarn to knit on large needles, whether you're recycling garments or buying new yardage. Knit the basic Buttonhole Bag pattern on page 25, omitting the buttonhole, and add handles to make a very large tote. The Bella bag has fewer stitches and rows, and so makes a smaller bag.

Tip

T-shirt fabric makes terrific bags with lots of stretch. Cut through the shirt below the sleeves to leave a tube, then cut around the tube in a spiral to make a continuous strip.

YOU WILL NEED

- Selection of plain, striped, and patterned cotton fabric
- Pair of size 17 (12 mm) knitting needles or size needed to achieve gauge
- Sewing thread and sewing needle

FINISHED SIZE

Bag measures 12 in. (30 cm) deep and 13 in. (33 cm) wide.

GAUGE

9 stitches and 14 rows to 4 in. (10 cm) over garter stitch.

PREPARING THE YARN

Make the fabric strips as shown (right).

KNITTING THE BAG

CO 26 sts.

Work even in garter stitch (knit every row) until the front measures 12 in. (30 cm), ending with a WS row. BO.

Work back to match front.

KNITTING THE HANDLES
(make two)

CO 7 sts. Work even in garter stitch until the handle measures 11 in. (28 cm), ending with a WS row. BO.

FINISHING THE BAG

Turn ends of fabric strips to wrong side and stitch them in place. Pin handles to wrong side of bag pieces, overlapping edges by about ³/₄ in. (2 cm). Stitch in place using double thread. Place front and back together with right sides facing and stitch together with an overcast seam using double thread. Turn to right side.

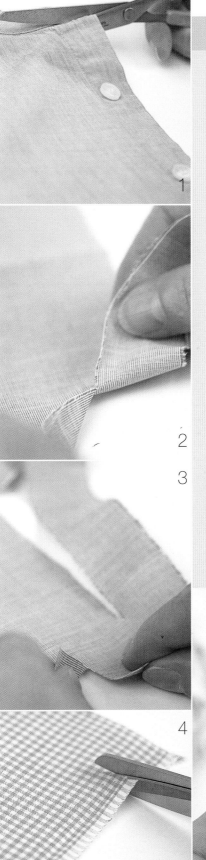

PREPARING THE YARN

1 If recycling shirt fabric, cut off collars, cuffs, and front bands, then trim away seams, hems, and excess fabric, leaving rectangular pieces of fabric. Press all fabric.

2 Lay piece of fabric on flat surface and cut a snip in bottom edge, about 1 in. (2.5 cm) from right-hand side. Holding both sides of snip firmly, tear fabric, stopping about 1 in. (2.5 cm) from top edge.

3 Turn fabric over so top edge is now at bottom. Cut a snip in this edge about 1 in. (2.5 cm) from previous tear and tear, again stopping 1 in. (2.5 cm) from fabric edge. Repeat across fabric, turning and tearing to make long continuous strip.

4 If using yardage rather than recycled fabric, tear strips in same way, but snip through selvedges that run lengthwise along edges of fabric. Tear strips across width of fabric rather than along length.

5 Roll fabric strips into balls, joining short edges as you add new strips to ball by overlapping ends and working couple of rows of small running stitches across strips to secure them.

candy

striped scarf

Simple stripes make the basic garter stitch Scarf into something fun to snuggle into on a cold winter's day. The stripes are worked in four randomly arranged colors, so one end of the scarf looks completely different to the other end.

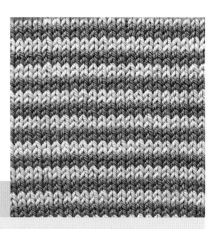

FUN WITH STRIPES

It's time to add some simple variations to your knitting repertoire. The easiest way to change a knit fabric is to introduce more colors. Horizontal stripes worked in two, three, or more colors add zing to plain garter or stockinette stitch accessories. The color choice is yours: stripe colors can contrast strongly or the effect can be made much more subtle by using a restricted palette of shades of one color plus one or more coordinating colors. Garter stitch, stockinette stitch, and rib patterns all look good worked in stripes.

REPEATING STRIPES

Worked in stockinette stitch, the narrow stripes are of identical widths and arranged in a repeating pattern. Work two rows in the main yarn and two rows in contrast yarn, then repeat the color sequence.

RANDOM STRIPES

Worked in stockinette stitch, these stripes are of different widths and arranged in a totally random color sequence. Work several rows in the main yarn, then continue working in the same stitch, changing colors at random after one, two, three, or more rows have been worked.

GARTER STRIPES

The appearance of stripes worked in garter stitch varies, depending on whether the first row of the new color starts on a right or wrong side row. On a right side row, the two yarns create a crisp line where the color changes. On a wrong side row, the two yarns interlock to give a broken line. To make the most of this effect, change colors after an odd number of rows have been worked. The sample was worked in three-row stripes.

SEQUENCED STRIPES

Worked in double rib, the narrow stripes repeat in a different way to those in the Repeating Stripes pattern. They are arranged to give a short stripe sequence separated by bands of the main yarn. Work in the main yarn to the required point, then work: 2 rows in contrast yarn A; 2 in contrast yarn B; 8 in main yarn; 2 in contrast yarn B; 2 rows in contrast yarn A. Continue in main yarn, repeating stripe sequence as required.

jolly

rib-stitch hat

This pretty hat is knit following the basic Hat pattern on page 27, but a lacy single eyelet rib is substituted for the ordinary double rib.

SINGLE EYELET RIB

This stitch pattern needs a multiple of 5 stitches plus 2.

Cast on the same number of stitches given in the basic Hat pattern (72 = 7 x 10 + 2).

ROWS 1 and 5: (RS) P2, * K3, P2; rep from * to end.

ROWS 2, 4, and 6: K2, * P3, K2; rep from * to end.

ROW 3: P2, * K2tog, YO, K1, P2; rep from * to end.

ROW 7: P2, * K1, YO, sl 1, K1, psso, P2; rep from * to end.

ROW 8: Rep Row 2.

Rep Rows 1 to 8 for length required.

SUBSTITUTING STITCHES

Stitch patterns need a given number of stitches on the needle for the pattern to work correctly. When using a different pattern to knit a scarf, simply cast on the number required and knit a long strip. To use a different stitch to knit a shaped accessory such as a hat, you'll need to choose a stitch that works over the same number of stitches, or adjust the number of stitches by adding or subtracting one or more.

After choosing your stitch pattern, cast on the correct number and work even until you reach the point where the shaping begins.

STITCHES

You can use any of these fancy rib stitches to knit our basic Hat from page 27. The instructions include calculations for casting on the correct number of stitches for each pattern.

DOUBLE EYELET RIB

This stitch pattern needs a multiple of 7 stitches plus 2.
Cast on the same number of stitches given in the basic Hat pattern (72 = 7 x 10 + 2).
ROW 1: (RS) P2, * K5, P2; rep from * to end.

ROW 2: K2, * P5, K2; rep from * to end.
ROW 3: P2, * K2tog, YO, K1, YO, sl 1, K1, psso, P2; rep from * to end.
ROW 4: Rep Row 2.
Rep Rows 1 to 4 for length required.

UNEVEN RIB

This stitch pattern needs a multiple of 4 stitches plus 3.
Cast on one stitch fewer than the number given in the basic Hat pattern (71 = 4 x 17 + 3).
ROW 1: * K2, P2; rep from * to last 3 sts, K2, P1.
Rep Row 1 for length required.

THREE-BY-ONE RIB

This stitch pattern needs a multiple of 4 stitches plus 1.
Cast on one more stitch than the number given in the basic Hat pattern (73 = 4 x 18 + 1).
ROW 1: (RS) K1, * P3, K1; rep from * to end.
ROW 2: P1, * K3, P1; rep from * to end.
Rep Rows 1 and 2 for length required.

THREE-BY-TWO RIB

This stitch pattern needs a multiple of 5 stitches plus 2.
Cast on the same number of stitches given in the basic Hat pattern (72 = 5 x 14 + 2).
ROW 1: (RS) P2, * K3, P2; rep from * to end.
ROW 2: K2, * P3, K2; rep from * to end.
Rep Rows 1 and 2 for length required.

fizzy

textured scarf

Novelty yarns make fabulous scarves that can add interest and color to a simple outfit. The Fizzy Scarf shown here was worked from the basic pattern on page 25 using one strand of double knitting yarn in pink held together with one strand of long eyelash yarn in variegated pink, white, lilac, and blue.

Tip

Novelty yarns work best with simple stitch patterns. Garter stitch makes a scarf reversible. Alternatively, knit in stockinette stitch to get a different texture on the right and wrong sides of your scarf.

WORKING WITH NOVELTY YARNS

Novelty yarns come in all sorts of textures, and can be a solid color or variegated. In small amounts they make decorative accents. Or you can replace a smooth yarn with a novelty yarn when knitting a project, providing the novelty yarn works up to the same gauge.

Many novelty yarns are made from a mixture of fibers and often need special care when washing. You'll usually find the fiber content and care details given on the ball or skein band. These yarns are a little difficult to work with because it's harder to distinguish the stitches than when knitting with smooth yarns. Concentrate and count carefully when casting on, binding off, and working increases and decreases.

The swatches shown provide an idea of the different types of novelty yarn you can buy. Each yarn is contrasted against a smooth chunky yarn made from pure wool. From top to bottom they are:

MOHAIR YARN

Mohair yarns are soft and fluffy and contain a high proportion of kid mohair spun around a synthetic core for strength. Some people find that mohair feels rather itchy next to their skin. You may prefer to use it in a band to trim the ends of a scarf, knitting the body of the scarf in a non-itchy wool or cotton yarn.

EYELASH YARN

Eyelash yarn comes in many varieties, and different effects are created by the length of the "lashes" radiating from a thin central core. This type of yarn is spun from synthetic fibers. Many eyelash yarns are a similar weight to double knitting yarn. Use them double or combined with one strand of a smooth yarn of similar weight to team them with chunky weight yarns.

NOVELTY WOOLEN YARN

Novelty yarns made from pure wool or wool/synthetic mixtures create a wide range of textures and color combinations. Yarns may be textured with loops, bobbles, and slubs, or be twisted to vary from very fine to very thick at regular intervals along the yarn. The yarn in the swatch is spun from pure wool and incorporates a kaleidoscope of bright colors.

SHORT EYELASH YARN

Short eyelash yarns have a different construction from the yarns described above. A length of short eyelash yarn is made from short fibers joined at one end to form a tiny fringe. This type of yarn has a soft, velvety feel and usually has a sheen.

fjord

felted bag

These two bags were knit
from the basic Buttonhole Bag
pattern on page 25 using
Icelandic Lopi wool. The pale
blue bag was washed hot
water, the dark blue bag was
not washed so is unfelted.

FELTING SWATCHES

Felting, or to give the process the correct
term, fulling, describes shrinking a piece
of knitted fabric so that it thickens and
becomes solid and fuzzy, yet still pliable.
Knitted felt usually shrinks more in length
than in width and the amount of shrinkage
will vary, depending on how loosely the
piece has been knitted.

The easiest way to felt something is to
machine wash it, adding an old towel or
pair of jeans to the machine for extra
friction. Pull the wet knitting gently into
shape and lay it flat to dry.

Pure wool yarns are used for felting,
but avoid those that are treated to be
machine washable, as most will not felt.
The best type to try are those wools
labeled as "hand wash only." Some yarns
lose stitch definition quickly when
washed, while others may need several
wash cycles before you get the effect you
want. Remember that felting is an inexact
science so always make a swatch and
wash and dry it first before starting to knit
your project. Keep on swatching until
you're happy with the results.

1 CHUNKY SHETLAND

Stockinette stitch worked in two colors of chunky Shetland wool and washed in hot water. The knit fabric has thickened up nicely, but there's still too much stitch definition at this stage.

2 THICK AND THIN WOOL

Stockinette stitch worked in a novelty, multicolored thick and thin yarn and washed in hot water. This yarn has felted a little bit too much, resulting in a hard, rather stiff fabric. It would be better washed at a lower temperature.

3 SHETLAND WOOL PLUS MOHAIR

Garter stitch worked in one strand of Shetland double knitting weight yarn plus one strand of mohair yarn and washed in hot water. This has a lovely finish; the stitch definition is still there, but the fabric has thickened up nicely. The mohair gives the felt a soft, furry surface.

4 TWO STRANDS OF MOHAIR

Stockinette stitch worked in one strand of solid color mohair yarn plus one strand of the same yarn in a variegated colorway and washed on a 60° wash. The felt feels thick and substantial, but is still very soft.

5 ICELANDIC WOOL

Garter stitch worked in Icelandic Lopi wool and washed in hot water. This type of wool felts really well, making a thick, even fabric. Dark colors may bleed during felting, so don't wash light and dark colors together.

victoria

hand-embroidered mittens

Sprinkle embroidered flowers across the back of stockinette stitch Mittens for a fresh feminine look. Choose a fairly dark color to knit the mittens, and embroider the flowers and leaves in bright shades of tapestry wool.

EMBROIDERY ON KNITTING

You've already learned how to do two stitches: backstitch (page 24) and blanket stitch along an edge (page 35). Backstitch makes a bold, solid line when worked onto the surface of knit fabric, while blanket stitch can be worked in rows or in a circle to add decoration. Two other useful stitches are shown on these pages: chain stitch and lazy daisy stitch. Use chain stitch to work heavy lines and lazy daisy stitch to make individual flower petals. Use tapestry wool or six strands of embroidery floss to work stitches onto chunky knitting, depending on the look you want to create.

WORKING A BLANKET STITCH ROW

1 Work blanket stitch as described on page 35, but work stitches on top of knit fabric and arrange them in a row.

WORKING CHAIN STITCH

1 Bring yarn through to right side, leaving yarn tail on surface. Take needle back through knitting close to where yarn emerged, and bring it back to right side short distance away.

2 Take working yarn under point of needle to make loop, then pull needle through to complete first stitch.

3 Repeat to make series of interlocking loops. At end of row, anchor last loop by making tiny straight stitch over it. Take yarn to wrong side and secure by weaving it through previous stitches. Anchor yarn tail in same way.

WORKING LAZY DAISY STITCH

1 This stitch is actually a single chain stitch. Bring needle through and make 1 chain stitch as above, then anchor loop with 1 tiny straight stitch.

2 Arrange subsequent stitches in circle to make flower shape, positioning each stitch to radiate outward from center point. Fasten off yarn after working each flower.

chapter 6
gallery

In this section you will find all the scarves, bags, mittens, hats, and

capelets made in the book. Glancing through these pages you will be able

to see the many **changes** and additions that were made to the five basic

patterns. Remember that the pieces shown can be made in **different**

colors to suit your particular style. Take the **beads** from a hat and use

them on mittens; keep the **handle** from a bag, but knit it in another yarn.

We hope you'll be inspired by the gallery to mix and match elements to

create your own, **completely original** accessories.

scarves

Basic Scarf, PAGE 25

Playful, PAGE 30

Scarf with pompoms

Weekend, PAGE 32

Scarf with simple fringe

Tab, PAGE 58

Scarf with tab-and-buckle fastening (right)

Sporty, PAGE 34

Scarf with blanket-stitch edging

Tuck, PAGE 54

Scarf with slit closure

Octopus, PAGE 56

Scarf with tie ends

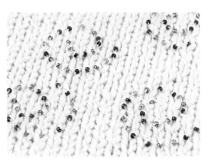

Swirl, PAGE 78

Scarf with beaded spirals

Firefly, PAGE 80

Scarf with knitted-in beads

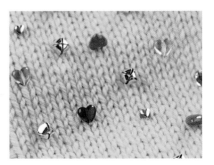

Charming, PAGE 82

Scarf with charms and bells

Candy, PAGE 106

Striped scarf

Bound scarf, PAGE 39

Scarf with fabric binding

Braided scarf, PAGE 73

Scarf with braids

Fizzy, PAGE 110

Textured scarf

Loopy scarf, PAGE 45

Scarf with French knit edge

Slashed scarf, PAGE 88

Felted slashed scarf

scarf variations

Lattice scarf, PAGE 33

Scarf with knotted fringe

Buttoned scarf, PAGE 67

Scarf with button-and-loop fastening

Beaded scarf, PAGE 99

Scarf with beaded fringe

Kinky scarf, PAGE 37

Scarf with curly fringe (left)

bags

Basic Buttonhole Bag, PAGE 25

Curly, PAGE 36

Bag with curly fringe

Violet, PAGE 38

Felted bag with fabric binding

Honey, PAGE 64

Bag with faux tortoiseshell handles (right)

Meadow, PAGE 42

Bag with felt appliqué flowers

Kate, PAGE 60

Bag with grab handles

Susie, PAGE 62

Felted bag with drawstring handles

Flora, PAGE 84

Bag with knitted ball buttons

Pearl, PAGE 86

Bag with mother-of-pearl buttons

Jenny, PAGE 88

Slashed felted bag

Bella, PAGE 104

Recycled fabric bag

Fjord, PAGE 112

Felted bag

bag variations

Pompom bag, PAGE 31

Felted bag with pompoms

Shoulder bag, PAGE 61

Bag with shoulder strap (right)

Fluffy bag, PAGE 51

Bag with marabou trim

Knotty bag, PAGE 57

Bag with ties

Buckled bag, PAGE 59

Bag with tab-and-buckle fastening

Zipper bag, PAGE 69

Bag with zippered pocket

Buttoned bag, PAGE 71

Bag with flap and cords

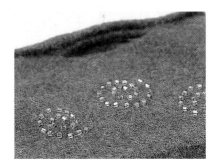

Spiral bag, PAGE 79

Felted bag with beads

Fringed bag, PAGE 95

Bag with beaded fringe

mittens

Basic Mittens, PAGE 26

Zippy, PAGE 68

Shortie mittens with zipper

Astra, PAGE 90

Mittens with starburst sequins

Froggy, PAGE 92

Mittens with novelty buttons

Julia, PAGE 41

Mittens with picot hem

Loopy, PAGE 66

Mittens with loop-and-button fastening

mitten variations

Dotty mittens, PAGE 43

Mittens with felt appliqué polka dots

Tasseled mittens, PAGE 49

Mittens with tassels

Foxy, PAGE 102

Long fingerless mittens

Pompom mittens, PAGE 63

Mittens with drawstring and pompoms

Victoria mittens, PAGE 114

Hand-embroidered mittens

Buttoned mittens, PAGE 84

Mittens with knitted buttons

hats

Basic Hat, PAGE 27

Paris, PAGE 44

Rib hat with French knit trim

Jaunty, PAGE 46

Rib hat with turn-back cuff

Swinger, PAGE 48

Rib hat with tassel

Anna, PAGE 70

Hat with earflaps and cords

Heidi, PAGE 72

Rib hat with braided ties

Gretchen, PAGE 94

Hat with beaded ties

Twinkle, PAGE 96

Hat with beaded brim

Jolly, PAGE 108

Rib-stitch hat

hat variations

Shamrock hat, PAGE 83

Hat with charms

Fishy Hat, PAGE 93

Hat with shank buttons

Swansdown, PAGE 50

Capelet with marabou trim

Bluebell, PAGE 74

Capelet with ribbon ties

capelets

Basic Capelet, PAGE 27

Senorita, PAGE 98

Capelet with beaded fringe

Index

Page numbers in italics refer to illustrations. As many of the same materials and techniques are used throughout the book, the page references are intended to direct the reader to substantial entries only.

Acknowledgments

Breslich & Foss Ltd and Jan Eaton would like to thank the following individuals for their help in the creation of this book: Nicola Hill for modeling the accessories and Jackie Jones for styling the hair and makeup; Pauline Hornsby for checking the patterns; Liz Marley for knitting many of the projects, and Martin Norris for photographing all the pieces. Last but not least, our thanks go to designer Elizabeth Healey, whose original concept this was.